FOR:

_____

To God belong wisdom and power;
counsel and understanding are his.

JOB 12:13

FROM:

_____

GOD'S
WORDS
OF LIFE
FOR MEN

ZONDERVAN®
.com

ZONDERVAN®

God's Words of Life for Men
Copyright © 1997 by Zondervan

Requests for information should be addressed to:
Zondervan, Grand Rapids, Michigan 49530

ISBN 978-0-310-33992-2

Excerpts taken from: Men's Devotional Bible, New International
Version. Copyright © 1993 by The Zondervan Corporation.

All Scripture quotations, unless otherwise indicated, are taken from
the Holy Bible: *New International Version*®. *NIV*®. Copyright © 1973,
1978, 1984, by Biblica, Inc.™ Used by permission. All rights reserved
worldwide.

Cover design/illustration: Greg Jackson-Thinpen Design

Printed in China

15 16 17 18 19 20 LEO 10 9 8 7 6 5 4

CONTENTS

GOD'S WORDS OF LIFE ON

GOD'S WORDS OF LIFE ON ANGER

My dear brothers, take note of this: Everyone should be quick to listen, slow to speak and slow to become angry, for man's anger does not bring about the righteous life that God desires.

JAMES 1:19–20

"In your anger do not sin": Do not let the sun go down while you are still angry, and do not give the devil a foothold.

EPHESIANS 4:26–27

A gentle answer turns away wrath,
but a harsh word stirs up anger.

PROVERBS 15:1

A patient man has great understanding,
but a quick-tempered man displays folly.

PROVERBS 14:29

Better a patient man than a warrior,
a man who controls his temper than one who
takes a city.

PROVERBS 16:32

Do not take revenge, my friends, but leave room for God's wrath, for it is written: "It is mine to avenge; I will repay," says the Lord. On the contrary: "If your enemy is hungry, feed him; if he is thirsty, give him something to drink. In doing this, you will heap burning coals on his head." Do not be overcome by evil, but overcome evil with good.

ROMANS 12:19–21

Get rid of all bitterness, rage and anger, brawling and slander, along with every form of malice. Be kind and compassionate to one another, forgiving each other, just as in Christ God forgave you.

EPHESIANS 4:31–32

But I tell you that anyone who is angry with his brother will be subject to judgment. . . . But anyone who says, "You fool!" will be in danger of the fire of hell.

MATTHEW 5:22

*A wise man fears the L*ORD *and shuns evil,*
 but a fool is hotheaded and reckless.
A quick-tempered man does foolish things,
 and a crafty man is hated.

PROVERBS 14:16–17

And he passed in front of Moses, proclaiming, "The LORD, the LORD, the compassionate and gracious God, slow to anger, abounding in love and faithfulness, maintaining love to thousands, and forgiving wickedness, rebellion and sin. Yet he does not leave the guilty unpunished; he punishes the children and their children for the sin of the fathers to the third and fourth generation."

EXODUS 34:6–7

But now you must rid yourselves of all such things as these: anger, rage, malice, slander, and filthy language from your lips.

COLOSSIANS 3:8

A hot-tempered man stirs up dissension,
 but a patient man calms a quarrel.

PROVERBS 15:18

*Starting a quarrel is like breaching a dam; so drop
the matter before a dispute breaks out.*

PROVERBS 17:14

*In your anger do not sin;
    when you are on your beds,
        search your hearts and be silent.*

PSALM 4:4

*Let the LORD judge the peoples.
Judge me, O LORD, according to my righteousness,
        according to my integrity, O Most High. . . .
My shield is God Most High,
    who saves the upright in heart.*

PSALM 7:8, 10

*Sing to the LORD, you saints of his;
    praise his holy name.
For his anger lasts only a moment,
    but his favor lasts a lifetime;
weeping may remain for a night,
    but rejoicing comes in the morning.*

PSALM 30:4–5

I will listen to what God the Lord will say;
  he promises peace to his people, his saints—
  but let them not return to folly.

Psalm 85:8

Though I walk in the midst of trouble,
  you preserve my life;
you stretch out your hand against the anger of my foes,
  with your right hand you save me.
The Lord will fulfill his purpose for me;
  your love, O Lord, endures forever—
  do not abandon the works of your hands.

Psalm 138:7–8

Do not make friends with a hot-tempered man,
  do not associate with one easily angered,
or you may learn his ways
  and get yourself ensnared.

Proverbs 22:24–25

I want men everywhere to lift up holy hands in prayer, without anger or disputing.

1 Timothy 2:8

Love is patient, love is kind. It does not envy, it does not boast, it is not proud. It is not rude, it is not self-seeking, it is not easily angered, it keeps no record of wrongs.

1 CORINTHIANS 13:4–5

Refrain from anger and turn from wrath;
*   do not fret—it leads only to evil.*

PSALM 37:8

If your enemy is hungry, give him food to eat;
*   if he is thirsty, give him water to drink.*
In doing this, you will heap burning coals on his
*   head,*
*   and the LORD will reward you.*

PROVERBS 25:21–22

An angry man stirs up dissension,
*   and a hot-tempered one commits many sins.*
A man's pride brings him low,
*   but a man of lowly spirit gains honor.*

PROVERBS 29:22–23

Who is a God like you,
who pardons sin and forgives the transgression
of the remnant of his inheritance?
You do not stay angry forever
but delight to show mercy.

MICAH 7:18

The LORD is compassionate and gracious,
slow to anger, abounding in love.
He will not always accuse,
nor will he harbor his anger forever.

PSALM 103:8–9

DEVOTIONAL THOUGHT ON ANGER

We live in an age of rage. By studying anger and its power, we can learn self-control so that we do not need to lose our temper in rage or abuse ourselves with resentment, but can defuse anger by resolving circumstances. We should reflect prayerfully about how we can incorporate these resolutions in our own lives:

- To keep my life centered on God, as best I can, recognizing that when I do not, my natural self will generate things to become angry about.
- To not condemn myself for feelings of anger.
- To do everything I can to avoid acting on the basis of anger.
- To clean up any problems I create as quickly as possible.
- To redirect the energy of anger away from hurting people and toward improving conditions for people.

Each person who has sought God's help in the understanding and resolution of his or her anger has, without exception, received that help. There is, indeed, a miracle involved. It is the miracle of God's love for us, the miracle of his redemptive grace.

Richard P. Walters

GOD'S WORDS OF LIFE ON
ANXIETY

Cast your cares on the LORD and he will sustain you;
he will never let the righteous fall.

PSALM 55:22

Commit your way to the LORD;
trust in him and he will do this:
He will make your righteousness shine like the dawn,
the justice of your cause like the noonday sun.

PSALM 37:5–6

Commit to the LORD whatever you do,
and your plans will succeed.

PROVERBS 16:3

Look at the birds of the air; they do not sow or reap or store away in barns, and yet your heavenly Father feeds them. Are you not much more valuable than they?

MATTHEW 6:26

Do not be anxious about anything, but in everything, by prayer and petition, with thanksgiving, present your requests to God. And the peace of God, which transcends all understanding, will guard your hearts and your minds in Christ Jesus.

PHILIPPIANS 4:6–7

Blessed is the man who trusts in the LORD, whose confidence is in him. He will be like a tree planted by the water that sends out its roots by the stream. It does not fear when heat comes; its leaves are always green. It has no worries in a year of drought and never fails to bear fruit.

JEREMIAH 17:7–8

Keep your lives free from the love of money and be content with what you have, because God has said, "Never will I leave you; never will I forsake you."

HEBREWS 13:5

The LORD himself goes before you and will be with you; he will never leave you nor forsake you. Do not be afraid; do not be discouraged.

DEUTERONOMY 31:8

Why do you worry about clothes? See how the lilies of the field grow. They do not labor or spin. Yet I tell you that not even Solomon in all his splendor was dressed like one of these. If that is how God clothes the grass of the field, which is here today and tomorrow is thrown into the fire, will he not much more clothe you, O you of little faith?

MATTHEW 6:28–30

Cast all your anxiety on him because he cares for you.

1 PETER 5:7

Then Jesus said to his disciples: "Therefore I tell you, do not worry about your life, what you will eat; or about your body, what you will wear. Life is more than food, and the body more than clothes."

LUKE 12:22–23

Do not worry about tomorrow, for tomorrow will worry about itself.

MATTHEW 6:34

But seek first [God's] kingdom and his righteousness, and all these things will be given to you as well.

MATTHEW 6:33

No one will be able to stand up against you all the days of your life. As I was with Moses, so I will be with you; I will never leave you nor forsake you.

JOSHUA 1:5

Be strong and courageous. Do not be terrified; do not be discouraged, for the LORD your God will be with you wherever you go.

JOSHUA 1:9

Be on your guard; stand firm in the faith; be men of courage; be strong.

1 CORINTHIANS 16:13

For God did not give us a spirit of timidity, but a spirit of power, of love and of self-discipline.

2 TIMOTHY 1:7

He who fears the LORD has a secure fortress,
and for his children it will be a refuge.

PROVERBS 14:26

Let us then approach the throne of grace with confidence, so that we may receive mercy and find grace to help us in our time of need.

HEBREWS 4:16

The LORD *is my shepherd, I shall not be in want.*
He makes me lie down in green pastures,
he leads me beside quiet waters,
he restores my soul.
He guides me in paths of righteousness
for his name's sake.
Even though I walk
through the valley of the shadow of death,
I will fear no evil,
for you are with me;
your rod and your staff,
they comfort me.
You prepare a table before me
in the presence of my enemies.
You anoint my head with oil;
my cup overflows.
Surely goodness and love will follow me
all the days of my life,
and I will dwell in the house of the LORD
forever.

PSALM 23:1–6

We say with confidence, "The Lord is my helper; I will not
be afraid."

HEBREWS 13:6

The LORD gives strength to his people;
the LORD blesses his people with peace.

PSALM 29:11

My flesh and my heart may fail,
but God is the strength of my heart
and my portion forever.

PSALM 73:26

Great peace have they who love God's law,
and nothing can make them stumble.

PSALM 119:165

Those who trust in the LORD are like Mount Zion,
which cannot be shaken but endures forever.

PSALM 125:1

I pray that out of his glorious riches he may strengthen you with power through his Spirit in your inner being, so that Christ may dwell in your hearts through faith. And I pray that you, being rooted and established in love, may have power, together with all the saints, to grasp how wide and long and high and deep is the love of Christ, and to know this love that surpasses knowledge—that you may be filled to the measure of all the fullness of God.

EPHESIANS 3:16–19

DEVOTIONAL THOUGHT ON ANXIETY

"Do not be anxious," Paul writes to the Philippians. In one sense it is like telling a woman with a bad head cold not to sniffle and sneeze. Or maybe it is more like telling a wino to lay off the booze or a compulsive gambler to stay away from the track.

Is anxiety a disease or an addiction? Perhaps it is something of both. Partly, perhaps, because you can't help it, and partly because for some dark reason you choose not to help it, you torment yourself with detailed visions of the worst that can possibly happen.

Paul does not deny that the worst things will happen finally to all of us, as indeed he must have had a strong suspicion they were soon to happen to him. He does not try to minimize them. He does not try to explain them away as God's will or God's judgment or God's method of testing our spiritual fiber. He simply tells the Philippians that in spite of them—even in the thick of them—they are to keep in constant touch with the One who unimaginably transcends the worst things as he also unimaginably transcends the best.

Frederick Buechner

GOD'S WORDS OF LIFE ON
AUTHENTIC MANHOOD

A man ought not to cover his head, since he is the image and glory of God; but the woman is the glory of man. For man did not come from woman, but woman from man; neither was man created for woman, but woman for man.

1 CORINTHIANS 11:7–9

Does not the very nature of things teach you that if a man has long hair, it is a disgrace to him, but that if a woman has long hair, it is her glory?

1 CORINTHIANS 11:14–15

When God created man, he made him in the likeness of God.

GENESIS 5:1

Yet, O LORD, you are our Father.
  We are the clay, you are the potter;
  we are all the work of your hand.

ISAIAH 64:8

You made man ruler over the works of your hands;
you put everything under his feet:
all flocks and herds,
and the beasts of the field,
the birds of the air,
and the fish of the sea,
all that swim the paths of the seas.
O LORD, our LORD,
how majestic is your name in all the earth!

PSALM 8:6–9

Then God said, "Let us make man in our image, in our likeness, and let them rule over the fish of the sea and the birds of the air, over the livestock, over all the earth, and over all the creatures that move along the ground." So God created man in his own image, in the image of God he created him; male and female he created them.

GENESIS 1:26–27

Be on your guard; stand firm in the faith; be men of courage; be strong. Do everything in love.

1 CORINTHIANS 16:13–14

If you have any encouragement from being united with Christ, if any comfort from his love, if any fellowship with the Spirit, if any tenderness and compassion, then make my joy complete by being like-minded, having the same love, being one in spirit and purpose. Do nothing out of selfish ambition or vain conceit, but in humility consider others better than yourselves. Each of you should look not only to your own interests, but also to the interests of others.

PHILIPPIANS 2:1–4

But when the time had fully come, God sent his Son, born of a woman, born under law, to redeem those under law, that we might receive the full rights of sons. Because you are sons, God sent the Spirit of his Son into our hearts, the Spirit who calls out, "Abba, Father." So you are no longer a slave, but a son; and since you are a son, God has made you also an heir.

GALATIANS 4:4–7

> *He has showed you, O man, what is good.*
>> *And what does the LORD require of you?*
> *To act justly and to love mercy*
>> *and to walk humbly with your God.*

MICAH 6:8

But there is a place where someone has testified: "What is man that you are mindful of him, the son of man that you care for him? You made him a little lower than the angels; you crowned him with glory and honor and put everything under his feet." In putting everything under him, God left nothing that is not subject to him. Yet at present we do not see everything subject to him.

HEBREWS 2:6–8

When the angel of the LORD appeared to Gideon, he said, "The LORD is with you, mighty warrior."

JUDGES 6:12

DEVOTIONAL THOUGHT ON AUTHENTIC MANHOOD

To a generation of men failed by their fathers and lost in a cloud of confusion, God says, "Don't spend a lifetime in aimless drifting. Don't succumb to mindless misinterpretations of masculine identity. Enter into a relationship with me, through Jesus Christ, and allow me to lead you into authentic manhood."

God wants us all to experience a deeper level of security. He wants emasculated men to become secure enough to confront timidity and fear, to take risks and make commitments. He wants macho men to become secure enough to crawl out from under the false pretensions and quit trying to impress people.

The freedom of authentic masculinity is an amazing thing to see. It produces a "divine elasticity" in men. Finally they can lead with firmness, then submit with humility. They can challenge with a cutting edge, then encourage with enthusiasm. They can fight aggressively for just causes, then moments later weep over suffering.

These are the masterpieces God had in mind when he created man. God looks at them and says, "Very good. You are magnificent creatures—and authentically male."

Bill Hybels

GOD'S WORDS OF LIFE ON
CARE

For I will give you words and wisdom that none of your adversaries will be able to resist or contradict.

LUKE 21:15

Every good and perfect gift is from above, coming down from the Father of the heavenly lights, who does not change like shifting shadows.

JAMES 1:17

But he said to me, "My grace is sufficient for you, for my power is made perfect in weakness." Therefore I will boast all the more gladly about my weaknesses, so that Christ's power may rest on me.

2 CORINTHIANS 12:9

For it is God who works in you to will and to act according to his good purpose.

PHILIPPIANS 2:13

I can do everything through him who gives me strength.

PHILIPPIANS 4:13

"This is the covenant I will make with the house of Israel
after that time," declares the LORD.
"I will put my law in their minds
and write it on their hearts.
I will be their God,
and they will be my people."

JEREMIAH 31:33

Not that we are competent in ourselves to claim anything for ourselves, but our competence comes from God.

2 CORINTHIANS 3:5

If you remain in me and my words remain in you, ask whatever you wish, and it will be given you.

JOHN 15:7

Praise be to the God and Father of our Lord Jesus Christ, who has blessed us in the heavenly realms with every spiritual blessing in Christ.

EPHESIANS 1:3

He who did not spare his own Son, but gave him up for us all—how will he not also, along with him, graciously give us all things?

ROMANS 8:32

Praise the LORD, O my soul,
and forget not all his benefits—
who forgives all your sins
and heals all your diseases,
who redeems your life from the pit
and crowns you with love and compassion,
who satisfies your desires with good things
so that your youth is renewed like the eagle's.

PSALM 103:2–5

Delight yourself in the LORD
and he will give you the desires of your heart.

PSALM 37:4

But whoever drinks the water I give him will never thirst. Indeed, the water I give him will become in him a spring of water welling up to eternal life.

JOHN 4:14

The eyes of all look to you,
*   and you give them their food at the proper time.*
You open your hand
*   and satisfy the desires of every living thing.*

PSALM 145:15–16

Praise be to the LORD, to God our Savior,
*   who daily bears our burdens.*

PSALM 68:19

Remember how the LORD your God led you all the way in the desert these forty years, to humble you and to test you in order to know what was in your heart, whether or not you would keep his commands.

DEUTERONOMY 8:2

For the eyes of the LORD range throughout the earth to strengthen those whose hearts are fully committed to him. You have done a foolish thing, and from now on you will be at war.

2 CHRONICLES 16:9

But you are a shield around me, O LORD;
*   you bestow glory on me and lift up my head.*

PSALM 3:3

Are not two sparrows sold for a penny? Yet not one of them will fall to the ground apart from the will of your Father. And even the very hairs of your head are all numbered. So don't be afraid; you are worth more than many sparrows.

MATTHEW 10:29–31

The LORD is my shepherd, I shall not be in want.
 He makes me lie down in green pastures,
he leads me beside quiet waters,
 he restores my soul.
He guides me in paths of righteousness
 for his name's sake.

PSALM 23:1–3

Because of the LORD's great love we are not consumed,
 for his compassions never fail.
They are new every morning;
 great is your faithfulness.
I say to myself, "The LORD is my portion;
 therefore I will wait for him."
The LORD is good to those whose hope is in him,
 to the one who seeks him;
it is good to wait quietly
 for the salvation of the LORD.

LAMENTATIONS 3:22–26

O LORD, you have searched me
and you know me.
You know when I sit and when I rise;
you perceive my thoughts from afar.
You discern my going out and my lying down;
you are familiar with all my ways. . . .
You hem me in—behind and before;
you have laid your hand upon me. . . .
Where can I go from your Spirit?
Where can I flee from your presence?
If I go up to the heavens, you are there;
if I make my bed in the depths, you are there.
If I rise on the wings of the dawn,
if I settle on the far side of the sea,
even there your hand will guide me,
your right hand will hold me fast. . . .
For you created my inmost being;
you knit me together in my mother's womb. . . .
My frame was not hidden from you
when I was made in the secret place.
When I was woven together in the depths of the
earth
your eyes saw my unformed body.

All the days ordained for me were written in
    your book
before one of them came to be.

PSALM 139:1–3, 5, 7–10, 13, 15–16

I love the LORD, for he heard my voice;
    he heard my cry for mercy.

PSALM 116:1

DEVOTIONAL THOUGHT ON CARE

I am progressing along the path of life in my ordinary con-tentedly fallen and godless condition, absorbed in a merry meeting with my friends for the morrow or a bit of work that tickles my vanity today, a holiday or a new book, when sud-denly a stab of abdominal pain that threatens serious disease, or a headline in the newspapers that threatens us all with destruction, sends this whole pack of cards tumbling down.

At first I am overwhelmed, and all my little happi-nesses look like broken toys. Then, slowly and reluctantly, bit by bit, I try to bring myself into the frame of mind that I should be in at all times.

I remind myself that all these toys were never intended to possess my heart, that my true good is in another world and my only real treasure is Christ. Perhaps, by God's grace, I succeed, and for a day or two become a creature consciously dependent on God and drawing its strength from the right sources.

But the moment the threat is withdrawn, my whole nature leaps back to the toys. . . . The terrible necessity of tribulation is only too clear . . . my only real treasure must be Christ.

C. S. Lewis

GOD'S WORDS OF LIFE ON
CHALLENGES

You will know that your children will be many,
and your descendants like the grass of the earth.
You will come to the grave in full vigor,
like sheaves gathered in season.

JOB 5:25–26

A man can do nothing better than to eat and drink and find satisfaction in his work. This too, I see, is from the hand of God, for without him, who can eat or find enjoyment? To the man who pleases him, God gives wisdom, knowledge and happiness, but to the sinner he gives the task of gathering and storing up wealth to hand it over to the one who pleases God. This too is meaningless, a chasing after the wind.

ECCLESIASTES 2:24–26

The LORD is upright;
he is my Rock, and there is no wickedness in him.

PSALM 92:15

I thought, "Age should speak; advanced years should teach wisdom." But it is the spirit in a man, the breath of the Almighty, that gives him understanding.

JOB 32:7–8

No one will be able to stand up against you all the days of your life. As I was with Moses, so I will be with you; I will never leave you nor forsake you.

JOSHUA 1:5

Even when I am old and gray,
do not forsake me, O God,
till I declare your power to the next generation,
your might to all who are to come.

PSALM 71:18

Young men and maidens,
old men and children.
Let them praise the name of the LORD,
for his name alone is exalted;
his splendor is above the earth and the heavens.

PSALM 148:12–13

*One thing I ask of the L*ORD,
*   this is what I seek:*
*that I may dwell in the house of the L*ORD
*   all the days of my life,*
*to gaze upon the beauty of the L*ORD
*   and to seek him in his temple.*

PSALM 27:4

Gray hair is a crown of splendor;
*   it is attained by a righteous life.*

PROVERBS 16:31

He has made everything beautiful in its time. He has also set eternity in the hearts of men; yet they cannot fathom what God has done from beginning to end.

ECCLESIASTES 3:11

Remember your Creator in the days of your youth, before the days of trouble come and the years approach when you will say, "I find no pleasure in them."

ECCLESIASTES 12:1

He asked you for life, and you gave it to him—
*   length of days, for ever and ever.*

PSALM 21:4

Even to your old age and gray hairs I am he,
I am he who will sustain you.
I have made you and I will carry you;
I will sustain you and I will rescue you.

ISAIAH 46:4

Man's days are determined;
you have decreed the number of his months
and have set limits he cannot exceed.

JOB 14:5

Honor your father and your mother, so that you may live
long in the land the LORD your God is giving you.

EXODUS 20:12

Whoever of you loves life
and desires to see many good days,
keep your tongue from evil
and your lips from speaking lies.

PSALM 34:12–13

With long life will I satisfy him
and show him my salvation.

PSALM 91:16

Keep my commands in your heart,
for they will prolong your life many years
and bring you prosperity.

PROVERBS 3:1–2

Through [God] your days will be many,
and years will be added to your life.

PROVERBS 9:11

The fear of the LORD adds length to life,
but the years of the wicked are cut short.

PROVERBS 10:27

Whoever would love life and see good days must keep his tongue from evil and his lips from deceitful speech. He must turn from evil and do good; he must seek peace and pursue it.

1 PETER 3:10–11

When I was a child, I talked like a child, I thought like a child, I reasoned like a child. When I became a man, I put childish ways behind me.

1 CORINTHIANS 13:11

As for man, his days are like grass,
he flourishes like a flower of the field.

PSALM 103:15

Finally, be strong in the Lord and in his mighty power. Put on the full armor of God so that you can take your stand against the devil's schemes. For our struggle is not against flesh and blood, but against the rulers, against the authorities, against the powers of this dark world and against the spiritual forces of evil in the heavenly realms. Therefore put on the full armor of God, so that when the day of evil comes, you may be able to stand your ground, and after you have done everything, to stand. Stand firm then, with the belt of truth buckled around your waist, with the breastplate of righteousness in place, and with your feet fitted with the readiness that comes from the gospel of peace. In addition to all this, take up the shield of faith, with which you can extinguish all the flaming arrows of the evil one. Take the helmet of salvation and the sword of the Spirit, which is the word of God.

EPHESIANS 6:10–17

DEVOTIONAL THOUGHT ON CHALLENGES

I have examined America's breathless lifestyle and find it to be unacceptable. At forty-three years of age (I would be forty-four but I was sick a year), I have been thinking about the stages of my earthly existence and what they will represent at its conclusion. There was a time when all of my friends were graduating from high school. Now, it occurs to me that a time will soon come when my friends will be dying.

What does this have to do with my life today? How does it relate to yours? I'm suggesting that we stop and consider the brevity of our years on earth, perhaps finding new motivation to preserve the values that will endure. Why should we work ourselves into an early grave, missing those precious moments with loved ones who crave our affection and attention? It is a question that every man and woman should consider.

Let me offer this final word of encouragement for those who are determined to slow the pace: once you get out from under constant pressure, you'll wonder why you drove yourself so hard for all those years.

James Dobson

So in everything, do to others what you would have them do to you, for this sums up the Law and the Prophets.

MATTHEW 7:12

Jesus replied: "'Love the Lord your God with all your heart and with all your soul and with all your mind.' This is the first and greatest commandment. And the second is like it: 'Love your neighbor as yourself.' All the Law and the Prophets hang on these two commandments."

MATTHEW 22:37–40

The entire law is summed up in a single command: "Love your neighbor as yourself."

GALATIANS 5:14

*Better a poor man whose walk is blameless
than a rich man whose ways are perverse.*

PROVERBS 28:6

LORD, who may dwell in your sanctuary?
    Who may live on your holy hill?
He whose walk is blameless
    and who does what is righteous,
    who speaks the truth from his heart
and has no slander on his tongue,
    who does his neighbor no wrong
    and casts no slur on his fellowman,
who despises a vile man
    but honors those who fear the LORD,
who keeps his oath even when it hurts,
    and does not change his mind.
who lends his money without usury
    and does not accept a bribe against the innocent.
He who does these things
    will never be shaken.

PSALM 15:1–5

Who may ascend the hill of the LORD?
    Who may stand in his holy place?
He who has clean hands and a pure heart,
    who does not lift up his soul to an idol
    or swear by what is false.

PSALM 24:3–4

He has showed you, O man, what is good.
And what does the LORD require of you?
To act justly and to love mercy
and to walk humbly with your God.

MICAH 6:8

But the fruit of the Spirit is love, joy, peace, patience, kindness, goodness, faithfulness, gentleness and self-control. Against such things there is no law.

GALATIANS 5:22–23

We also rejoice in our sufferings, because we know that suffering produces perseverance; perseverance, character; and character, hope.

ROMANS 5:3–4

Be careful that you do not forget the LORD your God, failing to observe his commands, his laws and his decrees.

DEUTERONOMY 8:11

See to it that no one misses the grace of God and that no bitter root grows up to cause trouble and defile many.

HEBREWS 12:15

This is what the Lord says:
"Stand at the crossroads and look;
*   ask for the ancient paths,*
ask where the good way is, and walk in it,
*   and you will find rest for your souls."*

JEREMIAH 6:16

We continually remember before our God and Father your work produced by faith, your labor prompted by love, and your endurance inspired by hope in our Lord Jesus Christ.

1 THESSALONIANS 1:3

Blessed is the man
*   who does not walk in the counsel of the wicked*
or stand in the way of sinners
*   or sit in the seat of mockers.*
But his delight is in the law of the Lord,
*   and on his law he meditates day and night.*
He is like a tree planted by streams of water,
*   which yields its fruit in season*
and whose leaf does not wither.
*   Whatever he does prospers.*

PSALM 1:1–3

Therefore, my dear friends, as you have always obeyed—not only in my presence, but now much more in my absence—continue to work out your salvation with fear and trembling, for it is God who works in you to will and to act according to his good purpose. Do everything without complaining or arguing so that you may become blameless and pure, children of God without fault in a crooked and depraved generation, in which you shine like stars in the universe.

PHILIPPIANS 2:12–15

Evil men do not understand justice,
but those who seek the LORD understand it fully.

PROVERBS 28:5

Young men be submissive to those who are older. All of you, clothe yourselves with humility toward one another, because, "God opposes the proud but gives grace to the humble."

1 PETER 5:5

But the noble man makes noble plans,
and by noble deeds he stands.

ISAIAH 32:8

My son, do not forget my teaching,
    but keep my commands in your heart,
for they will prolong your life many years
    and bring you prosperity.
Let love and faithfulness never leave you;
    bind them around your neck,
    write them on the tablet of your heart.
Then you will win favor and a good name
    in the sight of God and man.
Trust in the LORD with all your heart
    and lean not on your own understanding;
in all your ways acknowledge him,
    and he will make your paths straight.
Do not be wise in your own eyes;
    fear the LORD and shun evil.
This will bring health to your body
    and nourishment to your bones.

PROVERBS 3:1–8

The wisdom of the prudent is to give thought to
  their ways,
    but the folly of fools is deception.
Fools mock at making amends for sin,
    but goodwill is found among the upright.

PROVERBS 14:8–9

To the man who pleases him, God gives wisdom, knowledge and happiness, but to the sinner he gives the task of gathering and storing up wealth to hand it over to the one who pleases God. This too is meaningless, a chasing after the wind.

ECCLESIASTES 2:26

Dear friends, I urge you, as aliens and strangers in the world, to abstain from sinful desires, which war against your soul. Live such good lives among the pagans that, though they accuse you of doing wrong, they may see your good deeds and glorify God on the day he visits us.

1 PETER 2:11–12

And let us consider how we may spur one another on toward love and good deeds. Let us not give up meeting together, as some are in the habit of doing, but let us encourage one another—and all the more as you see the Day approaching.

HEBREWS 10:24–25

Love the LORD your God with all your heart and with all your soul and with all your strength. These commandments that I give you today are to be upon your hearts.

DEUTERONOMY 6:5–6

 Do to others as you would have them do to you.

LUKE 6:31

Consider it pure joy, my brothers, whenever you face trials of many kinds, because you know that the testing of your faith develops perseverance. Perseverance must finish its work so that you may be mature and complete, not lacking anything. If any of you lacks wisdom, he should ask God, who gives generously to all without finding fault, and it will be given to him. But when he asks, he must believe and not doubt, because he who doubts is like a wave of the sea, blown and tossed by the wind. That man should not think he will receive anything from the Lord; he is a double-minded man, unstable in all he does. . . . Blessed is the man who perseveres under trial, because when he has stood the test, he will receive the crown of life that God has promised to those who love him.

JAMES 1:2–8, 12

Do not merely listen to the word, and so deceive yourselves. Do what it says. Anyone who listens to the word but does not do what it says is like a man who looks at his face in a mirror and, after looking at himself, goes away and immediately forgets what he looks like. But the man who looks intently into the perfect law that gives freedom, and continues to do this, not forgetting what he has heard, but doing it—he will be blessed in what he does.

JAMES 1:22–25

DEVOTIONAL THOUGHT ON CHARACTER

Aristotle defined character as the decisions a person makes when the choice is not obvious. My father used to say, "Character is the way we act when nobody's looking."

For example, it's no test of character to stop your car at a police roadblock. The test comes, rather, when you're driving at 4 a.m. along a desolate back road in Iowa. You're heading toward a red light at a deserted intersection and you can see for miles around that there's nobody else on the roads. Do you obey the law, even though there's no cross traffic, or zoom on through at full speed? This is a test of character, a choice made on the basis of respect for law, on the discipline of adhering to the principles of safe driving. You decide to stop on the strength of character instead of responding to convenience or whim.

Of course, to the person who is well disciplined in respect for law, as well as other ethical and moral principles, such a simple illustration of choice is automatically invalid. For such a person, the only course of action is already established because you stop at red lights; that's all there is to it, whatever the time or traffic conditions. You do what is right, not what you know to be wrong.

D. Bruce Lockerbie

GOD'S WORDS OF LIFE ON
COMMITMENT

Again, you have heard that it was said to the people long ago, "Do not break your oath, but keep the oaths you have made to the Lord." But I tell you, Do not swear at all: either by heaven, for it is God's throne; or by the earth, for it is his footstool; or by Jerusalem, for it is the city of the Great King. And do not swear by your head, for you cannot make even one hair white or black. Simply let your "Yes" be "Yes," and your "No," "No"; anything beyond this comes from the evil one.

Matthew 5:33–37

Do not conform any longer to the pattern of this world, but be transformed by the renewing of your mind. Then you will be able to test and approve what God's will is—his good, pleasing and perfect will.

Romans 12:2

Whoever acknowledges me before men, I will also acknowledge him before my Father in heaven. But whoever disowns me before men, I will disown him before my Father in heaven.

MATTHEW 10:32–33

See, I am setting before you today a blessing and a curse—the blessing if you obey the commands of the LORD your God that I am giving you today; the curse if you disobey the commands of the LORD your God and turn from the way that I command you today by following other gods.

DEUTERONOMY 11:26–28

But Samuel replied: "Does the LORD delight in burnt offerings and sacrifices as much as in obeying the voice of the LORD? To obey is better than sacrifice, and to heed is better than the fat of rams."

1 SAMUEL 15:22

I am the true vine, and my Father is the gardener. He cuts off every branch in me that bears no fruit, while every branch that does bear fruit he prunes so that it will be even more fruitful. You are already clean because of the word I have spoken to you. Remain in me, and I will remain in you. No branch can bear fruit by itself; it must remain in the vine. Neither can you bear fruit unless you remain in me. I am the vine; you are the branches. If a man remains in me and I in him, he will bear much fruit; apart from me you can do nothing. If anyone does not remain in me, he is like a branch that is thrown away and withers; such branches are picked up, thrown into the fire and burned. If you remain in me and my words remain in you, ask whatever you wish, and it will be given you.

JOHN 15:1–7

I will give them singleness of heart and action, so that they will always fear me for their own good and the good of their children after them. I will make an everlasting covenant with them: I will never stop doing good to them, and I will inspire them to fear me, so that they will never turn away from me.

JEREMIAH 32:39–40

For I am convinced that neither death nor life, neither angels nor demons, neither the present nor the future, nor any powers, neither height nor depth, nor anything else in all creation, will be able to separate us from the love of God that is in Christ Jesus our Lord.

ROMANS 8:38–39

But when the kindness and love of God our Savior appeared, he saved us, not because of righteous things we had done, but because of his mercy. He saved us through the washing of rebirth and renewal by the Holy Spirit, whom he poured out on us generously through Jesus Christ our Savior, so that, having been justified by his grace, we might become heirs having the hope of eternal life. This is a trustworthy saying. And I want you to stress these things, so that those who have trusted in God may be careful to devote themselves to doing what is good. These things are excellent and profitable for everyone.

TITUS 3:4–8

DEVOTIONAL THOUGHT ON COMMITMENT

A well-known national television talk-show host once invited a minister of the gospel on his program. At one point the talk-show host asked the man of God why Christians were so narrow-minded in thinking that they were the only people in the whole world who knew God and who knew they were going to heaven.

The minister quoted scripture: "I am the way and the truth and the life. No one comes to the Father except through me" (John 14:6).

The preacher then stated, "I didn't say that, God did. If you don't agree with it, tell him, not me."

That's also the answer for training camp Christians [those who attempt to barter with God to achieve success]. The promises made, but not kept; the functions attended, but not experienced; the hopes dreamed, but not put into action—commitment matters. There is no success for a football player—or a Christian—without it.

Reggie White

GOD'S WORDS OF LIFE ON
COURAGE

The LORD is my light and my salvation—
whom shall I fear?
The LORD is the stronghold of my life—
of whom shall I be afraid?

PSALM 27:1

So do not fear, for I am with you;
do not be dismayed, for I am your God.
I will strengthen you and help you;
I will uphold you with my righteous right hand.

ISAIAH 41:10

Have I not commanded you? Be strong and courageous. Do not be terrified; do not be discouraged, for the LORD your God will be with you wherever you go.

JOSHUA 1:9

I can do everything through Christ who gives me strength.

PHILIPPIANS 4:13

Dear friends, do not be surprised at the painful trial you are suffering, as though something strange were happening to you. But rejoice that you participate in the sufferings of Christ, so that you may be overjoyed when his glory is revealed.

1 PETER 4:12–13

When you pass through the waters,
*   I will be with you;*
and when you pass through the rivers,
*   they will not sweep over you.*
When you walk through the fire,
*   you will not be burned;*
*   the flames will not set you ablaze.*
For I am the LORD, your God,
*   the Holy One of Israel, your Savior . . .*
you are precious and honored in my sight.

ISAIAH 43:2–4

No, in all these things we are more than conquerors through him who loved us. For I am convinced that neither death nor life, neither angels nor demons, neither the present nor the future, nor any powers, neither height nor depth, nor anything else in all creation, will be able to separate us from the love of God that is in Christ Jesus our Lord.

ROMANS 8:37–39

Wait for the LORD;
be strong and take heart
and wait for the LORD.

PSALM 27:14

How great is your goodness,
which you have stored up for those who fear you,
which you bestow in the sight of me
on those who take refuge in you.
In the shelter of your presence you hide them
from the intrigues of men;
in your dwelling you keep them safe
from accusing tongues. . . .
Be strong and take heart,
all you who hope in the LORD.

PSALM 31:19–20, 24

He gives strength to the weary
and increases the power of the weak.
Even youths grow tired and weary,
and young men stumble and fall;
but those who hope in the Lord
will renew their strength.
They will soar on wings like eagles;
they will run and not grow weary,
they will walk and not be faint.

ISAIAH 40:29–31

Do not be anxious about anything, but in everything, by prayer and petition, with thanksgiving, present your requests to God. And the peace of God, which transcends all understanding, will guard your hearts and your minds in Christ Jesus.

PHILIPPIANS 4:6–7

You will have success if you are careful to observe the decrees and laws that the Lord gave Moses for Israel. Be strong and courageous. Do not be afraid or discouraged.

1 CHRONICLES 22:13

Strengthen the feeble hands,
*   steady the knees that give way;*
say to those with fearful hearts,
*   "Be strong, do not fear;*
your God will come,
*   he will come with vengeance."*

ISAIAH 35:3–4

I have prayed for you . . . that your faith may not fail. And when you have turned back, strengthen your brothers.

LUKE 22:32

Be strong and very courageous. Be careful to obey all the law my servant Moses gave you; do not turn from it to the right or to the left, that you may be successful wherever you go.

JOSHUA 1:7

Be strong and courageous. Do not be afraid or terrified because of them, for the LORD your God goes with you; he will never leave you nor forsake you.

DEUTERONOMY 31:6

"I am about to go the way of all the earth," David said. "So be strong, show yourself a man, and observe what the LORD your God requires: Walk in his ways, and keep his decrees and commands, his laws and requirements, as written in the Law of Moses, so that you may prosper in all you do and wherever you go."

1 KINGS 2:2–3

Be strong in the Lord and in his mighty power.

EPHESIANS 6:10

Our fathers disciplined us for a little while as they thought best; but God disciplines us for our good, that we may share in his holiness. No discipline seems pleasant at the time, but painful. Later on, however, it produces a harvest of righteousness and peace for those who have been trained by it. Strengthen your feeble arms and weak knees. "Make level paths for your feet," so that the lame may not be disabled, but rather healed.

HEBREWS 12:10–13

But Jesus immediately said to them: "Take courage! It is I. Don't be afraid."

MATTHEW 14:27

Be on your guard; stand firm in the faith; be men of courage; be strong.

1 CORINTHIANS 16:13

Act with courage, and may the LORD be with those who do well.

2 CHRONICLES 19:11

For to me, to live is Christ and to die is gain.

PHILIPPIANS 1:21

I love you, O LORD, my strength.
The LORD is my rock, my fortress and my deliverer;
my God is my rock, in whom I take refuge.
He is my shield and the horn of my salvation,
my stronghold.

PSALM 18:1–2

DEVOTIONAL THOUGHT ON COURAGE

It takes courage to look your spouse in the eye and say, "Our marriage is in serious trouble, and we've got to do something about it."

What do most people do? They put their problems on the back burner and go their own directions. While they pursue their own careers and their own recreations, the marriage disintegrates from lack of courage. They did not have the courage to put on the gloves and say, "Let's fight for this marriage."

It takes courage to fight off the "greener grass" temptations, to work through layer after layer of masks, cover-ups, and defense mechanisms, to keep working on that marriage year after year. Relational courage does not apply only to the husband-wife relationship. . . .

It also takes relational courage to build significant relationships with friends, to look another person in the eye and say, "Isn't it time we stopped talking about the weather and the stock market and started talking about what's going on in your life and mine? Isn't it time we became brothers?"

Not many men have the courage to challenge each other, to fight for each other's spiritual and relational growth. But I have learned over the years that I will never be a success in my marriage, with my kids or with my friends, without courage.

Bill Hybels

GOD'S WORDS OF LIFE ON
DEPRESSION

You heard my cry for mercy
    when I called to you for help. . . .
Be strong and take heart,
    all you who hope in the LORD.

PSALM 31:22, 24

Cast your cares on the LORD
    and he will sustain you;
he will never let
    the righteous fall.

PSALM 55:22

Look at the birds of the air; they do not sow or reap or store away in barns, and yet your heavenly Father feeds them. Are you not much more valuable than they?

MATTHEW 6:26

I will refresh the weary and satisfy the faint.

JEREMIAH 31:25

Do not be anxious about anything, but in everything, by prayer and petition, with thanksgiving, present your requests to God. And the peace of God, which transcends all understanding, will guard your hearts and your minds in Christ Jesus.

PHILIPPIANS 4:6–7

In my distress I called to the LORD,
    and he answered me.
From the depths of the grave I called for help,
    and you listened to my cry.

JONAH 2:2

My tears have been my food
    day and night,
while men say to me all day long,
    "Where is your God?" . . .
Why are you downcast, O my soul?
    Why so disturbed within me?
Put your hope in God,
    for I will yet praise him,
    my Savior and my God.

PSALM 42:3, 5–6

Answer me quickly, O Lord;
my spirit fails.
Do not hide your face from me
or I will be like those who go down to the pit.
Let the morning bring me word of your unfailing love,
for I have put my trust in you.
Show me the way I should go,
for to you I lift up my soul.

PSALM 143:7–8

The Lord is a refuge for the oppressed,
a stronghold in times of trouble.

PSALM 9:9

The eternal God is your refuge, and underneath are the everlasting arms.

DEUTERONOMY 33:27

You are my lamp, O Lord; the Lord turns my darkness into light.

2 SAMUEL 22:29

A righteous man may have many troubles,
but the Lord delivers him from them all.

PSALM 34:19

If the LORD delights in a man's way,
    he makes his steps firm;
though he stumble, he will not fall,
    for the LORD upholds him with his hand.

PSALM 37:23–24

God is our refuge and strength,
    an ever-present help in trouble.
Therefore we will not fear, though the earth give way
    and the mountains fall into the heart of the sea,
though its waters roar and foam
    and the mountains quake with their surging.

PSALM 46:1–3

Though you have made me see troubles,
    many and bitter,
    you will restore my life again;
from the depths of the earth
    you will again bring me up.

PSALM 71:20

My flesh and my heart may fail,
    but God is the strength of my heart
    and my portion forever.

PSALM 73:26

Even youths grow tired and weary,
*   and young men stumble and fall;*
but those who hope in the LORD
*   will renew their strength.*
They will soar on wings like eagles;
*   they will run and not grow weary,*
*   they will walk and not be faint.*

ISAIAH 40:30–31

So do not fear, for I am with you;
*   do not be dismayed, for I am your God.*
I will strengthen you and help you;
*   I will uphold you with my righteous right hand.*

ISAIAH 41:10

When you pass through the waters,
*   I will be with you;*
and when you pass through the rivers,
*   they will not sweep over you.*
When you walk through the fire,
*   you will not be burned;*
*   the flames will not set you ablaze.*

ISAIAH 43:2

We are hard pressed on every side, but not crushed; perplexed, but not in despair; persecuted, but not abandoned; struck down, but not destroyed. . . . Therefore we do not lose heart. Though outwardly we are wasting away, yet inwardly we are being renewed day by day.

2 CORINTHIANS 4:8–9, 16

Jesus said, "I have told you these things, so that in me you may have peace. In this world you will have trouble. But take heart! I have overcome the world."

JOHN 16:33

> *As for God, his way is perfect;*
>   *the word of the LORD is flawless.*
>   *He is a shield for all who take refuge in him.*
> *For who is God besides the LORD?*
>   *And who is the Rock except our God?*
> *It is God who arms me with strength*
>   *and makes my way perfect.*
> *He makes my feet like the feet of a deer;*
>   *he enables me to stand on the heights.*

PSALM 18:30–33

Jesus answered "Do not let your hearts be troubled. Trust in God; trust also in me."

JOHN 14:1

Whenever anyone turns to the Lord, the veil is taken away. Now the Lord is the Spirit, and where the Spirit of the Lord is, there is freedom.

2 CORINTHIANS 3:16–17

But if you will look to God and plead with the Almighty, if you are pure and upright, even now he will rouse himself on your behalf and restore you to your rightful place.

JOB 8:5–6

Create in me a pure heart, O God,
*   and renew a steadfast spirit within me.*
Do not cast me from your presence
*   or take your Holy Spirit from me.*
Restore to me the joy of your salvation
*   and grant me a willing spirit, to sustain me.*

PSALM 51:10–12

DEVOTIONAL THOUGHT ON DEPRESSION

Life is always composed of those experiences and encounters which provide both challenge to one's character and the testing of one's spirit.

In 1 Kings 19, I see a defeated and desolate Elijah sitting under a broom tree in the solitude of his own sadness. He had to ask life's most difficult question: "How did I get to where I am which is so far from where I am supposed to be?"

I may as well tell you, there are only three kinds of people in the world: those who are in the wilderness, those who have just come out of the wilderness, and those who are headed into the wilderness. In the midst of Elijah's wilderness experience, God sent his angel to feed him. "You don't have enough for your journey."

"What journey? I'm through. I'm all washed up."

"You're not through yet, Elijah. I'm going to send you from where you are to where I want you to be. I'm going to send you from the wilderness to the mountain."

In the wilderness there is weakness, but on the mountain there is strength. In the wilderness there is loneliness, but on the mountain there is companionship. In the wilderness there is despair, but on the mountain there is hope.

H. Beecher Hicks

GOD'S WORDS OF LIFE ON
DISCIPLESHIP

Therefore, I urge you, brothers, in view of God's mercy, to offer your bodies as living sacrifices, holy and pleasing to God—this is your spiritual act of worship. Do not conform any longer to the pattern of this world, but be transformed by the renewing of your mind. Then you will be able to test and approve what God's will is—his good, pleasing and perfect will.

ROMANS 12:1–2

Blessed are those who are persecuted because of righteousness, for theirs is the kingdom of heaven. Blessed are you when people insult you, persecute you and falsely say all kinds of evil against you because of me. Rejoice and be glad, because great is your reward in heaven, for in the same way they persecuted the prophets who were before you. You are the salt of the earth. . . . You are the light of the world. . . . Let your light shine before men, that they may see your good deeds and praise your Father in heaven.

MATTHEW 5:10–14, 16

Anyone who loves his father or mother more than me is not worthy of me; anyone who loves his son or daughter more than me is not worthy of me; and anyone who does not take his cross and follow me is not worthy of me. Whoever finds his life will lose it, and whoever loses his life for my sake will find it.

MATTHEW 10:37–39

LORD, *who may dwell in your sanctuary?*
Who may live on your holy hill?
He whose walk is blameless
and who does what is righteous,
who speaks the truth from his heart.

PSALM 15:1–2

He who walks righteously
and speaks what is right,
who rejects gain from extortion
and keeps his hand from accepting bribes,
who stops his ears against plots of murder
and shuts his eyes against contemplating evil—
this is the man who will dwell on the heights.

ISAIAH 33:15–16

The fruit of righteousness will be peace;
*   the effect of righteousness will be quietness and*
*   confidence forever.*

ISAIAH 32:17

Is not this the kind of fasting I have chosen:
to loose the chains of injustice
*   and untie the cords of the yoke,*
to set the oppressed free
*   and break every yoke?*
Is it not to share your food with the hungry
*   and to provide the poor wanderer with shelter—*
when you see the naked, to clothe him,
*   and not to turn away from your own flesh and*
*   blood?*
Then your light will break forth like the dawn,
*   and your healing will quickly appear;*
*   then your righteousness will go before you,*
*   and the glory of the LORD will be your rear guard.*

ISAIAH 58:6–8

Those who live in accordance with the Spirit have their minds set on what the Spirit desires.

ROMANS 8:5

Remain in me, and I will remain in you. No branch can bear fruit by itself; it must remain in the vine. Neither can you bear fruit unless you remain in me. I am the vine; you are the branches. If a man remains in me and I in him, he will bear much fruit; apart from me you can do nothing.

JOHN 15:4–5

> He follows my decrees
>> and faithfully keeps my laws.
> That man is righteous;
>> he will surely live,
>>> declares the Sovereign LORD.

EZEKIEL 18:9

> He has showed you, O man, what is good.
>> And what does the LORD require of you?
> To act justly and to love mercy
>> and to walk humbly with your God.

MICAH 6:8

By this all men will know that you are my disciples, if you love one another.

JOHN 13:35

But whoever lives by the truth comes into the light, so that it may be seen plainly that what he has done has been done through God.

JOHN 3:21

Jesus replied, "If anyone loves me, he will obey my teaching. My Father will love him, and we will come to him and make our home with him."

JOHN 14:23

The one who sows to please the Spirit, from the Spirit will reap eternal life. Let us not become weary in doing good, for at the proper time we will reap a harvest if we do not give up.

GALATIANS 6:8–9

Everyone who hears these words of mine and puts them into practice is like a wise man who built his house on the rock. The rain came down, the streams rose, and the winds blew and beat against that house; yet it did not fall, because it had its foundation on the rock.

MATTHEW 7:24–25

But one thing I do: Forgetting what is behind and straining toward what is ahead, I press on toward the goal to win the prize for which God has called me heavenward in Christ Jesus.

PHILIPPIANS 3:13–14

The grace of God that brings salvation has appeared to all men. It teaches us to say "No" to ungodliness and worldly passions, and to live self-controlled, upright and godly lives in this present age.

TITUS 2:11–12

Religion that God our Father accepts as pure and faultless is this: to look after orphans and widows in their distress and to keep oneself from being polluted by the world.

JAMES 1:27

DEVOTIONAL THOUGHT ON DISCIPLESHIP

All my life I had made my football career the number-one priority and let it dictate the direction of my life. Now here in Matthew 7:24–25 the Bible was saying I needed to make God and his will first and follow his direction for my life.

The crossroads I faced in my life was really a spiritual crossroads. I had to decide whether or not I believed what the Bible said. All my other questions hung on that one decision. But I finally reached a point where faith outweighed the doubts, and I was willing to commit my entire life to God.

I can't say that decision made an immediately visible difference in my life. I can't even say it instantly transformed me into a much better person; I had a lot yet to learn—and I still do—about how God wants me to live my life.

But what my new Christian experience did for me was to place football behind the priorities of my faith and my family and give me a sense of confidence and peace about the future—whatever it would be.

Tom Landry

GOD'S WORDS OF LIFE ON
EGO

I denied myself nothing my eyes desired; I refused my heart no pleasure. My heart took delight in all my work, and this was the reward for all my labor. Yet when I surveyed all that my hands had done and what I had toiled to achieve, everything was meaningless, a chasing after the wind; nothing was gained under the sun.

ECCLESIASTES 2:10–11

If you love those who love you, what credit is that to you? Even "sinners" love those who love them. And if you do good to those who are good to you, what credit is that to you? Even "sinners" do that. And if you lend to those from whom you expect repayment, what credit is that to you? Even "sinners" lend to "sinners," expecting to be repaid in full. But love your enemies, do good to them, and lend to them without expecting to get anything back. Then your reward will be great, and you will be sons of the Most High.

LUKE 6:32–35

Be on your guard; stand firm in the faith; be men of courage; be strong. Do everything in love.

1 CORINTHIANS 16:13–14

Now this is what the LORD Almighty says: "Give careful thought to your ways."

HAGGAI 1:5

Therefore, I urge you, brothers, in view of God's mercy, to offer your bodies as living sacrifices, holy and pleasing to God—this is your spiritual act of worship. Do not conform any longer to the pattern of this world, but be transformed by the renewing of your mind. Then you will be able to test and approve what God's will is—his good, pleasing and perfect will.

ROMANS 12:1–2

We who are strong ought to bear with the failings of the weak and not to please ourselves. Each of us should please his neighbor for his good, to build him up.

ROMANS 15:1–2

Nobody should seek his own good, but the good of others.

1 CORINTHIANS 10:24

Carry each other's burdens, and in this way you will fulfill the law of Christ. If anyone thinks he is something when he is nothing, he deceives himself.

GALATIANS 6:2–3

Each of you should look not only to your own interests, but also to the interests of others. Your attitude should be the same as that of Christ Jesus.

PHILIPPIANS 2:4–5

If anyone has material possessions and sees his brother in need but has no pity on him, how can the love of God be in him? Dear children, let us not love with words or tongue but with actions and in truth.

1 JOHN 3:17–18

Love is patient, love is kind. It does not envy, it does not boast, it is not proud. It is not rude, it is not self-seeking, it is not easily angered, it keeps no record of wrongs.

1 CORINTHIANS 13:4–5

If you really keep the royal law found in Scripture, "Love your neighbor as yourself," you are doing right.

JAMES 2:8

Even youths grow tired and weary,
 and young men stumble and fall;
but those who hope in the Lord
 will renew their strength.
They will soar on wings like eagles;
 they will run and not grow weary,
 they will walk and not be faint.

Isaiah 40:30–31

DEVOTIONAL THOUGHT ON EGO

You meet so many small men! Not small in stature—but men who think little, talk little, plan little. Like eagles staked to the ground, there's no soar to them. Ceiling is zero—and their horizons are pulled in to the hub.

Not that these men are selfish (some of course are). But it's just that they're preoccupied most of the time with their own little bailiwick. They don't allow their minds to stretch and breathe. They don't think—they just rearrange their prejudices.

These little men are indifferent to problems other than their own. They have no concern for those things which do not hold a personal reference. They refuse to be bothered!

The times demand big men. Not men who are big shots (they're useless), but men who are big in heart and mind. Great men! Large-souled men!

Men with a vision—whose feet are on the ground but whose eyes are on the far horizon. Men whose hearts God has touched. Men committed—dedicated to God and his holy, high purposes! Men of integrity!

Richard Halverson

GOD'S WORDS OF LIFE ON
ETERNAL LIFE

And this is the testimony: God has given us eternal life, and this life is in his Son.

1 JOHN 5:11

Jesus said "I tell you the truth, whoever hears my word and believes him who sent me has eternal life and will not be condemned; he has crossed over from death to life."

JOHN 5:24

For God so loved the world that he gave his one and only Son, that whoever believes in him shall not perish but have eternal life.

JOHN 3:16

Jesus answered, "I tell you the truth, he who believes has everlasting life."

JOHN 6:47

Jesus said, "But whoever drinks the water I give him will never thirst. Indeed, the water I give him will become in him a spring of water welling up to eternal life."

JOHN 4:14

We know that the Son of God has come and has given us understanding, so that we may know him who is true. And we are in him who is true—even in his Son Jesus Christ. He is the true God and eternal life.

1 JOHN 5:20

Surely goodness and love will follow me
    all the days of my life,
and I will dwell in the house of the LORD
    forever.

PSALM 23:6

Therefore, my brothers, I want you to know that through Jesus the forgiveness of sins is proclaimed to you. Through him everyone who believes is justified from everything you could not be justified from by the law of Moses.

ACTS 13:38–39

Jesus said to her, "I am the resurrection and the life. He who believes in me will live, even though he dies; and whoever lives and believes in me will never die."

JOHN 11:25–26

Praise be to the God and Father of our Lord Jesus Christ! In his great mercy he has given us new birth into a living hope through the resurrection of Jesus Christ from the dead.

1 PETER 1:3

If you confess with your mouth, "Jesus is Lord," and believe in your heart that God raised him from the dead, you will be saved. For it is with your heart that you believe and are justified, and it is with your mouth that you confess and are saved. As the Scripture says, "Anyone who trusts in him will never be put to shame." For there is no difference between Jew and Gentile—the same Lord is Lord of all and richly blesses all who call on him, for, "Everyone who calls on the name of the Lord will be saved."

ROMANS 10:9–13

Jesus answered, "My sheep listen to my voice; I know them, and they follow me. I give them eternal life, and they shall never perish; no one can snatch them out of my hand."

JOHN 10:27–28

Then know this, you and all the people of Israel: It is by the name of Jesus Christ of Nazareth, whom you crucified but whom God raised from the dead, that this man stands before you healed. He is "the stone you builders rejected, which has become the capstone. Salvation is found in no one else, for there is no other name under heaven given to men by which we must be saved."

ACTS 4:10–12

DEVOTIONAL THOUGHT ON ETERNAL LIFE

Father of glory,

How I thank you for the assurance of heaven! While I know I could never deserve such an assurance, I'm so grateful that you even give it to me as a right because of my union with your Son, my Savior.

Thank you that while I live in the world I can seek to serve you fruitfully, and to praise you by the kind of life I live, as well as by my lips. I long to give glory, honor and thanks to you always.

May your indwelling Spirit—the Spirit of glory—ever keep before me the great privilege of being an heir of your glory, and a citizen of heaven. May my life in its praise and worship of you now be the closest possible approximation to the praise and worship of heaven.

Father, I worship and adore you, through Jesus Christ your Son.

Amen.

Derek Prime

GOD'S WORDS OF LIFE ON FAILURE

David said to Solomon his son, "Be strong and courageous, and do the work. Do not be afraid or discouraged, for the LORD God, my God, is with you. He will not fail you or forsake you."

1 CHRONICLES 28:20

Because of the LORD's great love we are not consumed,
for his compassions never fail.
They are new every morning;
great is your faithfulness.

LAMENTATIONS 3:22–23

But he said to me, "My grace is sufficient for you, for my power is made perfect in weakness." Therefore I will boast all the more gladly about my weaknesses, so that Christ's power may rest on me.

2 CORINTHIANS 12:9

For we do not have a high priest who is unable to sympathize with our weaknesses, but we have one who has been tempted in every way, just as we are—yet was without sin. Let us then approach the throne of grace with confidence, so that we may receive mercy and find grace to help us in our time of need.

HEBREWS 4:15–16

> The LORD is good,
>   a refuge in times of trouble.
> He cares for those who trust in him.

NAHUM 1:7

> When you pass through the waters,
>   I will be with you;
> and when you pass through the rivers,
>   they will not sweep over you.
> When you walk through the fire,
>   you will not be burned;
>   the flames will not set you ablaze.

ISAIAH 43:2

[God] will remain faithful, for he cannot disown himself.

2 TIMOTHY 2:13

Though I walk in the midst of trouble,
You O Lord preserve my life;
you stretch out your hand against the anger of my foes,
with your right hand you save me.

Psalm 138:7

Praise be to the God and Father of our Lord Jesus Christ, the Father of compassion and the God of all comfort, who comforts us in all our troubles, so that we can comfort those in any trouble with the comfort we ourselves have received from God.

2 Corinthians 1:3–4

For everything that was written in the past was written to teach us, so that through endurance and the encouragement of the Scriptures we might have hope.

Romans 15:4

And we know that in all things God works for the good of those who love him, who have been called according to his purpose.

Romans 8:28

I lift up my eyes to the hills—
  where does my help come from?
*My help comes from the L*ORD,
  the Maker of heaven and earth.

PSALM 121:1–2

Do not conform any longer to the pattern of this world, but be transformed by the renewing of your mind. Then you will be able to test and approve what God's will is—his good, pleasing and perfect will.

ROMANS 12:2

All this is for your benefit, so that the grace that is reaching more and more people may cause thanksgiving to overflow to the glory of God. Therefore we do not lose heart. Though outwardly we are wasting away, yet inwardly we are being renewed day by day. For our light and momentary troubles are achieving for us an eternal glory that far outweighs them all. So we fix our eyes not on what is seen, but on what is unseen. For what is seen is temporary, but what is unseen is eternal.

2 CORINTHIANS 4:15–18

DEVOTIONAL THOUGHT ON FAILURE

It would be a tragedy if my kids grew up knowing only that their dad was a good football player and husband and father. If they thought I expected them to live every minute of their lives the way they have seen me live as they grew up, they would be frustrated and devastated if they ever failed. I want them to know what they didn't see, when I failed miserably and only came out of it by the grace of God.

As they get older and able to understand, I'm committed to being open and honest with them. I want them to know of my mistakes so they can avoid them. I also want them to know of my mistakes because they will make their own, and I don't want them to feel they are the first person in the family to fail.

I want to be able to sit with my kids and tell them some of the things I have done. Not to glorify sin. Not to justify it. Not to say everybody does it so it must be okay. Rather, because I'm not proud of it and because I don't want them to feel unique. Most of all, I want them to know that by the grace of God, he brought me through it and out of it, and he can do the same for them.

Mike Singletary

Make every effort to add to your faith goodness; and to goodness, knowledge; and to knowledge, self-control; and to self-control, perseverance; and to perseverance, godliness; and to godliness, brotherly kindness; and to brotherly kindness, love. For if you possess these qualities in increasing measure, they will keep you from being ineffective and unproductive in your knowledge of our Lord Jesus Christ.

2 PETER 1:5–8

Abram believed the LORD, and he credited it to him as righteousness.

GENESIS 15:6

Consequently, faith comes from hearing the message, and the message is heard through the word of Christ.

ROMANS 10:17

For by the grace given me I say to every one of you: Do not think of yourself more highly than you ought, but rather think of yourself with sober judgment, in accordance with the measure of faith God has given you.

ROMANS 12:3

"Have faith in God," Jesus answered. "I tell you the truth, if anyone says to this mountain, 'Go, throw yourself into the sea,' and does not doubt in his heart but believes that what he says will happen, it will be done for him. Therefore I tell you, whatever you ask for in prayer, believe that you have received it, and it will be yours."

MARK 11:22–24

Let us fix our eyes on Jesus, the author and perfecter of our faith, who for the joy set before him endured the cross, scorning its shame, and sat down at the right hand of the throne of God.

HEBREWS 12:2

Jesus replied, "Because you have so little faith. I tell you the truth, if you have faith as small as a mustard seed, you can say to this mountain, 'Move from here to there' and it will move. Nothing will be impossible for you."

MATTHEW 17:20

For in the gospel a righteousness from God is revealed, a righteousness that is by faith from first to last, just as it is written: "The righteous will live by faith."

ROMANS 1:17

I have been crucified with Christ and I no longer live, but Christ lives in me. The life I live in the body, I live by faith in the Son of God, who loved me and gave himself for me.

GALATIANS 2:20

And without faith it is impossible to please God, because anyone who comes to him must believe that he exists and that he rewards those who earnestly seek him.

HEBREWS 11:6

These have come so that your faith—of greater worth than gold, which perishes even though refined by fire—may be proved genuine and may result in praise, glory and honor when Jesus Christ is revealed. Though you have not seen him, you love him; and even though you do not see him now, you believe in him and are filled with an inexpressible and glorious joy, for you are receiving the goal of your faith, the salvation of your souls.

1 PETER 1:7–9

Just then a woman . . . came up behind him and touched the edge of his cloak. She said to herself, "If I only touch his cloak, I will be healed." Jesus turned and saw her. "Take heart, daughter," he said, "your faith has healed you." And the woman was healed from that moment.

MATTHEW 9:20–22

Jesus said "According to your faith will it be done to you."

MATTHEW 9:29

Now faith is being sure of what we hope for and certain of what we do not see.

HEBREWS 11:1

I tell you the truth, anyone who has faith in me will do what I have been doing. He will do even greater things than these, because I am going to the Father. And I will do whatever you ask in my name, so that the Son may bring glory to the Father. You may ask me for anything in my name, and I will do it.

JOHN 14:12–14

We live by faith, not by sight.

2 CORINTHIANS 5:7

To the man who does not work but trusts God who justifies the wicked, his faith is credited as righteousness.

ROMANS 4:5

Therefore, since we have been justified through faith, we have peace with God through our Lord Jesus Christ, through whom we have gained access by faith into this grace in which we now stand. And we rejoice in the hope of the glory of God.

ROMANS 5:1–2

Be on your guard; stand firm in the faith; be men of courage; be strong.

1 CORINTHIANS 16:13

For it is by grace you have been saved, through faith—and this not from yourselves, it is the gift of God—not by works, so that no one can boast.

EPHESIANS 2:8–9

For though I am absent from you in body, I am present with you in spirit and delight to see how orderly you are and how firm your faith in Christ is. So then, just as you received Christ Jesus as Lord, continue to live in him, rooted and built up in him, strengthened in the faith as you were taught, and overflowing with thankfulness.

COLOSSIANS 2:5–7

DEVOTIONAL THOUGHT ON FAITH

God was perfect and I wasn't. I was just a guy, and he was, well, God. How could I relate to him? A friend named Butch said Jesus was the answer. I could relate to him because even though he was perfect, he had also become a man. He was the bridge. He paid for my sin. If I could accept that and believe in Christ, then I could be forgiven and know I was going to heaven.

Overnight I pulled out the Gideon Bible. My mind was racing. Do I believe in God? Yes. Do I believe the Bible is God's message to man? Yes. Do I believe what the Bible says? Yes. That all have sinned? Yes. Do I want to become a Christian? How does one go about praying? I didn't know. I figured if God was God, he would understand if I just told him what was on my mind.

I said, "God, I don't know everything about you. I don't think I ever will. But I know I'm a sinner and I know I want to be forgiven. I know I want Christ in my life, and I want to go to heaven. I want to become a Christian. With that, I accept you. Amen." No tears, no lightning, no wind, no visions. What a relief! I knew I had done the right thing. I had stepped from skepticism to belief.

Orel Hershiser

GOD'S WORDS OF LIFE ON
FAITHFULNESS

And he passed in front of Moses, proclaiming, "The LORD, the LORD, the compassionate and gracious God, slow to anger, abounding in love and faithfulness."

EXODUS 34:6

Your love, O LORD, reaches to the heavens,
your faithfulness to the skies.

PSALM 36:5

God sends his love and his faithfulness. . . .
I will praise you, O LORD, among the nations;
I will sing of you among the peoples.
For great is your love, reaching to the heavens;
your faithfulness reaches to the skies.

PSALM 57:3, 9–10

Now it is required that those who have been given a trust must prove faithful.

1 CORINTHIANS 4:2

I put in charge of Jerusalem my brother Hanani, along with Hananiah the commander of the citadel, because he was a man of integrity and feared God more than most men do.

NEHEMIAH 7:2

Who then is the faithful and wise servant, whom the master has put in charge of the servants in his household to give them their food at the proper time? It will be good for that servant whose master finds him doing so when he returns. I tell you the truth, he will put him in charge of all his possessions.

MATTHEW 24:45–47

He will cover you with his feathers,
and under his wings you will find refuge;
his faithfulness will be your shield and rampart.

PSALM 91:4

Let love and faithfulness never leave you;
bind them around your neck,
write them on the tablet of your heart.
Then you will win favor and a good name
in the sight of God and man.

PROVERBS 3:3–4

For the LORD is good and his love endures forever;
his faithfulness continues through all generations.

PSALM 100:5

My eyes will be on the faithful in the land,
that they may dwell with me;
he whose walk is blameless
will minister to me.

PSALM 101:6

They could find no corruption in [Daniel], because he was trustworthy and neither corrupt nor negligent.

DANIEL 6:4

His master replied, "Well done, good and faithful servant! You have been faithful with a few things; I will put you in charge of many things. Come and share your master's happiness!"

MATTHEW 25:21

But the fruit of the Spirit is love, joy, peace, patience, kindness, goodness, faithfulness, gentleness and self-control.

GALATIANS 5:22–23

A faithful man will be richly blessed,
but one eager to get rich will ~~not~~ BE go unpunished.

PROVERBS 28:20

For I have kept the ways of the LORD; I have not done evil by turning from my God. All his laws are before me; I have not turned away from his decrees. I have been blameless before him and have kept myself from sin. The LORD has rewarded me according to my righteousness, according to my cleanness in his sight. To the faithful you show yourself faithful, to the blameless you show yourself blameless.

2 SAMUEL 22:22–26

Yet this I call to mind
and therefore I have hope:
Because of the LORD's great love we are not consumed,
for his compassions never fail.
They are new every morning;
great is your faithfulness.

LAMENTATIONS 3:21–23

DEVOTIONAL THOUGHT ON FAITHFULNESS

Biblical friendship calls for faithfulness. Circumstances should not affect our consistency. In Romans 12:15 Paul tells us to "rejoice with those who rejoice; mourn with those who mourn."

Faithfulness is critical to a close relationship because we depend on those who are close to us. Christ's deepest hurts occurred within his circle of closest companions, and David was wounded emotionally more by the treachery of his close friends than by the efforts of his enemies (Psalm 55:12–14). Paul too was left to stand alone when he was deserted by Demas and others (2 Timothy 4:10).

A faithful friend keeps confidences. In Proverbs we read that "a perverse man stirs up dissension, and a gossip separates close friends" (16:28). Entering friendship involves revealing yourself in confidence to another, and thus becoming vulnerable. This is as it should be, but it is what makes betrayal so evil and faithfulness so virtuous.

David W. Smith

GOD'S WORDS OF LIFE ON FINANCES

The LORD is my shepherd, I shall not be in want.

PSALM 23:1

No one can serve two masters. Either he will hate the one and love the other, or he will be devoted to the one and despise the other. You cannot serve both God and Money.

MATTHEW 6:24

Whoever trusts in his riches will fall,
but the righteous will thrive like a green leaf.

PROVERBS 11:28

I know what it is to be in need, and I know what it is to have plenty. I have learned the secret of being content in any and every situation, whether well fed or hungry, whether living in plenty or in want.

PHILIPPIANS 4:12

But godliness with contentment is great gain. For we brought nothing into the world, and we can take nothing out of it. But if we have food and clothing, we will be content with that. People who want to get rich fall into temptation and a trap and into many foolish and harmful desires that plunge men into ruin and destruction. For the love of money is a root of all kinds of evil. Some people, eager for money, have wandered from the faith and pierced themselves with many griefs.

1 TIMOTHY 6:6–10

Jesus sat down opposite the place where the offerings were put and watched the crowd putting their money into the temple treasury. Many rich people threw in large amounts. But a poor widow came and put in two very small copper coins, worth only a fraction of a penny. Calling his disciples to him, Jesus said, "I tell you the truth, this poor widow has put more into the treasury than all the others. They all gave out of their wealth; but she, out of her poverty, put in everything—all she had to live on."

MARK 12:41–44

And my God will meet all your needs according to his glorious riches in Christ Jesus.

PHILIPPIANS 4:19

Will a man rob God? Yet you rob me. But you ask, "How do we rob you?" In tithes and offerings. You are under a curse—the whole nation of you—because you are robbing me. Bring the whole tithe into the storehouse, that there may be food in my house. Test me in this, says the LORD Almighty, and see if I will not throw open the floodgates of heaven and pour out so much blessing that you will not have room enough for it.

MALACHI 3:8–10

Then Jesus said to them, "Watch out! Be on your guard against all kinds of greed; a man's life does not consist in the abundance of his possessions."

LUKE 12:15

Keep your lives free from the love of money and be content with what you have, because God has said, "Never will I leave you; never will I forsake you."

HEBREWS 13:5

Make it your ambition to lead a quiet life, to mind your own business and to work with your hands, just as we told you, so that your daily life may win the respect of outsiders and so that you will not be dependent on anybody.

1 THESSALONIANS 4:11–12

So do not worry, saying, "What shall we eat?" or "What shall we drink?" or "What shall we wear?" For the pagans run after all these things, and your heavenly Father knows that you need them. But seek first his kingdom and his righteousness, and all these things will be given to you as well.

MATTHEW 6:31–33

Let no debt remain outstanding, except the continuing debt to love one another, for he who loves his fellowman has fulfilled the law.

ROMANS 13:8

Do not let this Book of the Law depart from your mouth; meditate on it day and night, so that you may be careful to do everything written in it. Then you will be prosperous and successful.

JOSHUA 1:8

A good man leaves an inheritance for his children's children, but a sinner's wealth is stored up for the righteous.

PROVERBS 13:22

But remember the LORD your God, for it is he who gives you the ability to produce wealth, and so confirms his covenant, which he swore to your forefathers, as it is today.

DEUTERONOMY 8:18

Jesus looked at him and loved him. "One thing you lack," he said. "Go, sell everything you have and give to the poor, and you will have treasure in heaven. Then come, follow me." At this the man's face fell. He went away sad, because he had great wealth.

MARK 10:21–22

And God is able to make all grace abound to you, so that in all things at all times, having all that you need, you will abound in every good work.

2 CORINTHIANS 9:8

But store up for yourselves treasures in heaven, where moth and rust do not destroy, and where thieves do not break in and steal. For where your treasure is, there your heart will be also.

MATTHEW 6:20–21

If they obey and serve [God],
> *they will spend the rest of their days in prosperity*
> *and their years in contentment.*

JOB 36:11

Give, and it will be given to you. A good measure, pressed down, shaken together and running over, will be poured into your lap. For with the measure you use, it will be measured to you.

LUKE 6:38

DEVOTIONAL THOUGHT ON FINANCES

Never settle for second-rate or selfish goals. Set goals for yourself that involve helping other people and the riches will follow.

The richest people I know are those who have given themselves unselfishly to other people. Such motivation will affect the way you sell, cook, teach or ply your particular trade.

True riches, of course, are totally unrelated to money or material reward. In fact, if a person has earned money without helping people, his money will not buy him happiness.

Of one thing I am sure: happy people have strong goals—and somehow these include helping other people. They can also be assured that they will never run out of people to help.

Tim LaHaye

GOD'S WORDS OF LIFE ON FORGIVENESS

You forgave the iniquity of your people
and covered all their sins.

PSALM 85:2

As far as the east is from the west,
so far has God removed our transgressions
from us.

PSALM 103:12

My dear children, I write this to you so that you will not sin. But if anybody does sin, we have one who speaks to the Father in our defense—Jesus Christ, the Righteous One.

1 JOHN 2:1

If we confess our sins, God is faithful and just and will forgive us our sins and purify us from all unrighteousness.

1 JOHN 1:9

And when you stand praying, if you hold anything against anyone, forgive him, so that your Father in heaven may forgive you your sins.

MARK 11:25

Forgive whatever grievances you may have against one another. Forgive as the Lord forgave you.

COLOSSIANS 3:13

The Lord said, "I will cleanse them from all the sin they have committed against me and will forgive all their sins of rebellion against me."

JEREMIAH 33:8

> O LORD, hear my voice.
> Let your ears be attentive
>   to my cry for mercy.
> If you, O LORD, kept a record of sins,
>   O LORD, who could stand?
> But with you there is forgiveness;
>   therefore you are feared.
> I wait for the LORD, my soul waits,
>   and in his word I put my hope.

PSALM 130:2–5

"Come now, let us reason together,"
says the LORD.
"Though your sins are like scarlet,
they shall be as white as snow;
though they are red as crimson,
they shall be like wool."

ISAIAH 1:18

When you were dead in your sins and in the uncircumcision of your sinful nature, God made you alive with Christ. He forgave us all our sins.

COLOSSIANS 2:13

"I, even I, am he who blots out
your transgressions, for my own sake,
and remembers your sins no more."

ISAIAH 43:25

In him we have redemption through his blood, the forgiveness of sins, in accordance with the riches of God's grace.

EPHESIANS 1:7

Jesus said, "I tell you the truth, all the sins and blasphemies of men will be forgiven them."

MARK 3:28

Blessed is he
    whose transgressions are forgiven,
    whose sins are covered.
Blessed is the man
    whose sin the Lord does not count against him
    and in whose spirit is no deceit.

PSALM 32:1–2

Let the wicked forsake his way
    and the evil man his thoughts.
Let him turn to the Lord, and he will have mercy
    on him,
    and to our God, for he will freely pardon.

ISAIAH 55:7

Once you were alienated from God and were enemies in your minds because of your evil behavior. But now he has reconciled you by Christ's physical body through death to present you holy in God's sight, without blemish and free from accusation.

COLOSSIANS 1:21–22

Blessed are they whose transgressions are forgiven, whose sins are covered.

ROMANS 4:7

If my people, who are called by my name, will humble themselves and pray and seek my face and turn from their wicked ways, then will I hear from heaven and will forgive their sin and will heal their land.

2 CHRONICLES 7:14

"I will forgive their wickedness and will remember their sins no more."

HEBREWS 8:12

Then Peter came to Jesus and asked, "Lord, how many times shall I forgive my brother when he sins against me? Up to seven times?" Jesus answered, "I tell you, not seven times, but seventy-seven times."

MATTHEW 18:21–22

Do not judge, and you will not be judged. Do not condemn, and you will not be condemned. Forgive, and you will be forgiven. Give, and it will be given to you. A good measure, pressed down, shaken together and running over, will be poured into your lap. For with the measure you use, it will be measured to you.

LUKE 6:37–38

Peter replied, "Repent and be baptized, every one of you, in the name of Jesus Christ for the forgiveness of your sins. And you will receive the gift of the Holy Spirit. The promise is for you and your children and for all who are far off—for all whom the Lord our God will call."

ACTS 2:38–39

Help us, O God our Savior,
for the glory of your name;
deliver us and forgive our sins
for your name's sake.

PSALM 79:9

For if you forgive men when they sin against you, your heavenly Father will also forgive you. But if you do not forgive men their sins, your Father will not forgive your sins.

MATTHEW 6:14–15

Be kind and compassionate to one another, forgiving each other, just as in Christ God forgave you.

EPHESIANS 4:32

DEVOTIONAL THOUGHT ON FORGIVENESS

Forgiving is love's revolution against love's unfairness. When we forgive, we ignore the normal laws that strap us to the natural law of getting even and, by the alchemy of love, we release ourselves from our own painful pasts.

We fly over a dues-paying morality in order to create a new future out of the past's unfairness. We free ourselves from the wrong that is locked into our private histories.

We unshackle our spirits from malice; and, maybe, if we are lucky, we also restore a relationship that would otherwise be lost forever.

Lewis B. Smedes

GOD'S WORDS OF LIFE ON FRIENDSHIP

A friend loves at all times,
and a brother is born for adversity.

PROVERBS 17:17

Jesus said, "I no longer call you servants, because a servant does not know his master's business. Instead, I have called you friends, for everything that I learned from my Father I have made known to you."

JOHN 15:15

A despairing man should have the devotion of his
*   friends,*
*   even though he forsakes the fear of the Almighty.*

JOB 6:14

My intercessor is my friend
*   as my eyes pour out tears to God.*

JOB 16:20

                                     113

He who covers over an offense promotes love,
>   but whoever repeats the matter separates close
>   friends.

PROVERBS 17:9

A man of many companions may come to ruin,
>   but there is a friend who sticks closer than a
>   brother.

PROVERBS 18:24

Two are better than one,
>   because they have a good return for their work:
If one falls down,
>   his friend can help him up.
But pity the man who falls
>   and has no one to help him up!

ECCLESIASTES 4:9–10

Do not make friends with a hot-tempered man,
>   do not associate with one easily angered,
or you may learn his ways
>   and get yourself ensnared.

PROVERBS 22:24–25

Wounds from a friend can be trusted.

PROVERBS 27:6

Jesus said, "Greater love has no one than this, that he lay down his life for his friends. You are my friends if you do what I command."

JOHN 15:13–14

Perfume and incense bring joy to the heart,
and the pleasantness of one's friend
springs from his earnest counsel.

PROVERBS 27:9

Also, if two lie down together, they will keep warm. But how can one keep warm alone? Though one may be overpowered, two can defend themselves. A cord of three strands is not quickly broken.

ECCLESIASTES 4:11–12

The LORD would speak to Moses face to face, as a man speaks with his friend.

EXODUS 33:11

He who loves a pure heart and whose speech is gracious
will have the king for his friend.

PROVERBS 22:11

A righteous man is cautious in friendship,
but the way of the wicked leads them astray.

PROVERBS 12:26

A perverse man stirs up dissension,
and a gossip separates close friends.

PROVERBS 16:28

He who covers over an offense promotes love,
but whoever repeats the matter separates close friends.

PROVERBS 17:9

Jonathan had David reaffirm his oath out of love for him, because he loved him as he loved himself.

1 SAMUEL 20:17

DEVOTIONAL THOUGHT ON FRIENDSHIP

One of the finest examples of male friendship is found in the historical record of 1 Samuel. Here we read about real male friendship, about a relationship that ran deep between Jonathan, the king's son, and David, a shepherd boy and God's future choice for the throne. Their friendship was strong, built solidly on an inward attachment rather than on an outer attraction or social status. These men demonstrated a mutual acceptance of each other despite their different social backgrounds. David's interests were more important to Jonathan than his own, and David felt the same way about Jonathan's interests.

If you study the friendship between David and Jonathan, you will walk away with a good understanding of what a healthy friendship between men can and should be. Any definition should include the following:

- Unconditional love
- Personal enjoyment
- Mutual acceptance
- Mutual interests

- Mutual commitment
- Mutual loyalty

In short, friendship involves a concern for and involvement with the well-being of another.

David W. Smith

GOD'S WORDS OF LIFE ON
GRIEF AND DEATH

If only for this life we have hope in Christ, we are to be pitied more than all men. But Christ has indeed been raised from the dead, the firstfruits of those who have **fallen** asleep. For since death came through a man, the resurrection of the dead comes also through a man. For as in Adam all die, so in Christ all will be made alive.

1 CORINTHIANS 15:19–22

Listen, I tell you a mystery: We will not all sleep, but we will all be changed—in a flash, in the twinkling of an eye, at the last trumpet. For the trumpet will sound, the dead will be raised imperishable, and we will be changed. For the perishable must clothe itself with the imperishable, and the mortal with immortality. When the perishable has been clothed with the imperishable, and the mortal with immortality, then the saying that is written will come true: "Death has been swallowed up in victory." "Where, O death, is your victory? Where, O death, is your sting?"

1 CORINTHIANS 15:51–55

We believe that Jesus died and rose again and so we believe that God will bring with Jesus those who have fallen asleep in him. According to the Lord's own word, we tell you that we who are still alive, who are left till the coming of the Lord, will certainly not precede those who have fallen asleep. For the Lord himself will come down from heaven, with a loud command, with the voice of the archangel and with the trumpet call of God, and the dead in Christ will rise first. After that, we who are still alive and are left will be caught up together with them in the clouds to meet the Lord in the air. And so we will be with the Lord forever.

1 THESSALONIANS 4:14–18

The LORD brings death and makes alive; he brings down to the grave and raises up.

1 SAMUEL 2:6

And I heard a loud voice from the throne saying, "Now the dwelling of God is with men, and he will live with them. They will be his people, and God himself will be with them and be their God. He will wipe every tear from their eyes. There will be no more death or mourning or crying or pain, for the old order of things has passed away."

REVELATION 21:3–4

Even though I walk
through the valley of the shadow of death,
I will fear no evil,
for you are with me;
your rod and your staff,
they comfort me.

PSALM 23:4

Into your hands I commit my spirit;
redeem me, O LORD, the God of truth.

PSALM 31:5

You guide me with your counsel,
and afterward you will take me into glory.
Whom have I in heaven but you?
And earth has nothing I desire besides you.
My flesh and my heart may fail,
but God is the strength of my heart and my
portion forever.

PSALM 73:24–26

Precious in the sight of the LORD
is the death of his saints.

PSALM 116:15

Those who walk uprightly
enter into peace;
they find rest as they lie in death.

ISAIAH 57:2

For none of us lives to himself alone and none of us dies to himself alone. If we live, we live to the Lord; and if we die, we die to the Lord. So, whether we live or die, we belong to the Lord.

ROMANS 14:7–8

Now we know that if the earthly tent we live in is destroyed, we have a building from God, an eternal house in heaven, not built by human hands.

2 CORINTHIANS 5:1

[Christ] died for us so that, whether we are awake or asleep, we may live together with him.

1 THESSALONIANS 5:10

For to me, to live is Christ and to die is gain.

PHILIPPIANS 1:21

Now there is in store for me the crown of righteousness, which the Lord, the righteous Judge, will award to me on that day—and not only to me, but also to all who have longed for his appearing.

2 TIMOTHY 4:8

Since the children have flesh and blood, he too shared in their humanity so that by his death he might destroy him who holds the power of death—that is, the devil—and free those who all their lives were held in slavery by their fear of death.

HEBREWS 2:14–15

Then I heard a voice from heaven say, "Blessed are the dead who die in the Lord from now on." "Yes," says the Spirit, "they will rest from their labor, for their deeds will follow them."

REVELATION 14:13

But if Christ is in you, your body is dead because of sin, yet your spirit is alive because of righteousness. And if the Spirit of him who raised Jesus from the dead is living in you, he who raised Christ from the dead will also give life to your mortal bodies through his Spirit, who lives in you.

ROMANS 8:10–11

For I am convinced that neither death nor life, neither angels nor demons, neither the present nor the future, nor any powers, neither height nor depth, nor anything else in all creation, will be able to separate us from the love of God that is in Christ Jesus our Lord.

ROMANS 8:38–39

My comfort in my suffering is this:
    Your promise preserves my life.

PSALM 119:50

But the eyes of the LORD are on those who fear him,
    on those whose hope is in his unfailing love,
to deliver them from death
    and keep them alive in famine.
We wait in hope for the LORD;
    he is our help and our shield.
In him our hearts rejoice,
    for we trust in his holy name.
May your unfailing love rest upon us, O LORD,
    even as we put our hope in you.

PSALM 33:18–22

Blessed are those who mourn, for they will be comforted.

MATTHEW 5:4

He will swallow up death forever.
The Sovereign LORD will wipe away the tears
    from all faces;
he will remove the disgrace of his people
    from all the earth.
        The LORD has spoken.

ISAIAH 25:8

DEVOTIONAL THOUGHT ON GRIEF AND DEATH

How much faith is enough in our mourning? Some of us feel that it is always more than what we have.

Jesus said that the amount of faith isn't important. If we have faith, though it be as small as a mustard seed, nothing will be impossible.

I interpret faith in this instance as basic trust. We don't need a huge quantity of it in order to get on with our bereavement. In fact, if we worry about having a lot of faith, we may miss the mustard seed we do have.

The giver of this grain of faith is God, whose Son maintained his faith. He went through his Gethsemane of grief with the word "Father" still on his lips.

We too can go through the valleys and mountains of our bereavement journey with "Father" on our lips. Our hearts may wonder, doubt and cry out in pain, but these feelings will not obliterate our faith. Even when we think we have lost that mustard seed, we do well to remember that our Father is faithful, for he has loved us first.

Philip W. Williams

GOD'S WORDS OF LIFE ON
HOLINESS

It is the LORD your God you must follow, and him you must revere. Keep his commands and obey him; serve him and hold fast to him.

DEUTERONOMY 13:4

Therefore, I urge you, brothers, in view of God's mercy, to offer your bodies as living sacrifices, holy and pleasing to God—this is your spiritual act of worship. Do not conform any longer to the pattern of this world, but be transformed by the renewing of your mind. Then you will be able to test and approve what God's will is—his good, pleasing and perfect will.

ROMANS 12:1–2

Make every effort to live in peace with all men and to be holy; without holiness no one will see the Lord.

HEBREWS 12:14

What does the LORD your God ask of you but to fear the LORD your God, to walk in all his ways, to love him, to serve the LORD your God with all your heart and with all your soul.

DEUTERONOMY 10:12

Serve him with wholehearted devotion and with a willing mind, for the LORD searches every heart and understands every motive behind the thoughts. If you seek him, he will be found by you; but if you forsake him, he will reject you forever.

1 CHRONICLES 28:9

By dying to what once bound us, we have been released from the law so that we serve in the new way of the Spirit, and not in the old way of the written code.

ROMANS 7:6

But Samuel replied: "Does the LORD delight in burnt offerings and sacrifices as much as in obeying the voice of the LORD? To obey is better than sacrifice, and to heed is better than the fat of rams."

1 SAMUEL 15:22

God did not call us to be impure, but to live a holy life.

1 THESSALONIANS 4:7

If only you had paid attention to my commands,
your peace would have been like a river,
your righteousness like the waves of the sea.

ISAIAH 48:18

Obey me, and I will be your God and you will be my people. Walk in all the ways I command you, that it may go well with you.

JEREMIAH 7:23

But be very careful to keep the commandment and the law that Moses the servant of the LORD gave you: to love the LORD your God, to walk in all his ways, to obey his commands, to hold fast to him and to serve him with all your heart and all your soul.

JOSHUA 22:5

But now that you have been set free from sin and have become slaves to God, the benefit you reap leads to holiness, and the result is eternal life.

ROMANS 6:22

Since we have these promises, dear friends, let us purify ourselves from everything that contaminates body and spirit, perfecting holiness out of reverence for God.

2 CORINTHIANS 7:1

Our people must learn to devote themselves to doing what is good, in order that they may provide for daily necessities and not live unproductive lives.

TITUS 3:14

He has raised up a horn of salvation for us in the house of his servant David . . . to rescue us from the hand of our enemies, and to enable us to serve him without fear in holiness and righteousness before him all our days.

LUKE 1:69, 74–75

May he strengthen your hearts so that you will be blameless and holy in the presence of our God and Father when our Lord Jesus comes with all his holy ones.

1 THESSALONIANS 3:13

But just as he who called you is holy, so be holy in all you do; for it is written: "Be holy, because I am holy."

1 PETER 1:15–16

Therefore, brothers, since we have confidence to enter the Most Holy Place by the blood of Jesus, by a new and living way opened for us through the curtain, that is, his body, and since we have a great priest over the house of God, let us draw near to God with a sincere heart in full assurance of faith, having our hearts sprinkled to cleanse us from a guilty conscience and having our bodies washed with pure water. Let us hold unswervingly to the hope we profess, for he who promised is faithful. And let us consider how we may spur one another on toward love and good deeds. Let us not give up meeting together, as some are in the habit of doing, but let us encourage one another—and all the more as you see the Day approaching.

HEBREWS 10:19–25

Therefore, since we are receiving a kingdom that cannot be shaken, let us be thankful, and so worship God acceptably with reverence and awe, for our "God is a consuming fire."

HEBREWS 12:28–29

Ascribe to the LORD, O families of nations, ascribe to the LORD glory and strength, ascribe to the LORD the glory due his name. Bring an offering and come before him; worship the LORD in the splendor of his holiness.

1 CHRONICLES 16:28–29

I will show my greatness and my holiness, and I will make myself known in the sight of many nations. Then they will know that I am the LORD.

EZEKIEL 38:23

Our fathers disciplined us for a little while as they thought best; but God disciplines us for our good, that we may share in his holiness.

HEBREWS 12:10

It is because of him that you are in Christ Jesus, who has become for us wisdom from God—that is, our righteousness, holiness and redemption.

1 CORINTHIANS 1:30

DEVOTIONAL THOUGHT ON HOLINESS

One of the more serious sins of Christians today may well be the almost flippant familiarity with which we often address God in prayer. None of the godly men of the Bible ever adopted the casual manner we often do.

In our day we must begin to recover a sense of awe and profound reverence for God. We must begin to view him once again in the infinite majesty that alone belongs to him who is the Creator and Supreme Ruler of the entire universe. There is an infinite gap in worth and dignity between God the Creator and man the creature, even though man has been created in the image of God. The fear of God is a heartfelt recognition of this gap—not a put-down of man, but an exaltation of God.

We seem to have magnified the love of God almost to the exclusion of the fear of God. Because of this preoccupation we are not honoring God and reverencing him as we should. We should magnify the love of God; but although we revel in his love and mercy, we must never lose sight of his majesty and his holiness.

Jerry Bridges

Be strong and take heart,
all you who hope in the LORD.

PSALM 31:24

But the eyes of the LORD are on those who fear him,
on those whose hope is in his unfailing love.

PSALM 33:18

May your unfailing love rest upon us, O LORD,
even as we put our hope in you.

PSALM 33:22

I wait for you, O LORD;
you will answer, O LORD my God.

PSALM 38:15

But now, LORD, what do I look for?
My hope is in you.

PSALM 39:7

Why are you downcast, O my soul?
    Why so disturbed within me?
Put your hope in God,
    for I will yet praise him,
    my Savior and my God.

PSALM 43:5

For you have been my hope, O Sovereign LORD,
    my confidence since my youth.

PSALM 71:5

But as for me, I will always have hope;
    I will praise God more and more.

PSALM 71:14

May those who fear God rejoice when they see me,
    for I have put my hope in your word.

PSALM 119:74

Sustain me according to your promise, and I
    will live; do not let my hopes be dashed.

PSALM 119:116

Put your hope in the LORD,
  for with the LORD is unfailing love
  and with him is full redemption.

PSALM 130:7

Blessed is he whose help is the God of Jacob,
  whose hope is in the LORD his God,
the Maker of heaven and earth,
  the sea, and everything in them—
  the LORD, who remains faithful forever.

PSALM 146:5–6

Hope deferred makes the heart sick,
  but a longing fulfilled is a tree of life.

PROVERBS 13:12

Know also that wisdom is sweet to your soul;
  if you find it, there is a future hope for you,
  and your hope will not be cut off.

PROVERBS 24:14

But blessed is the man who trusts in the LORD,
  whose confidence is in him.

He will be like a tree planted by the water
that sends out its roots by the stream.
It does not fear when heat comes;
its leaves are always green.
It has no worries in a year of drought
and never fails to bear fruit.

JEREMIAH 17:7–8

Yet this I call to mind
and therefore I have hope:
Because of the LORD's great love we are not
consumed,
for his compassions never fail.

LAMENTATIONS 3:21–22

I say to myself, "The LORD is my portion;
therefore I will wait for him."
The LORD is good to those whose hope is in him,
to the one who seeks him.

LAMENTATIONS 3:24–25

We also rejoice in our sufferings, because we know that suffering produces perseverance; perseverance, character;

and character, hope. And hope does not disappoint us, because God has poured out his love into our hearts by the Holy Spirit, whom he has given us.

ROMANS 5:3–5

For in this hope we were saved. But hope that is seen is no hope at all. Who hopes for what he already has? But if we hope for what we do not yet have, we wait for it patiently.

ROMANS 8:24–25

For everything that was written in the past was written to teach us, so that through endurance and the encouragement of the Scriptures we might have hope.

ROMANS 15:4

May the God of hope fill you with all joy and peace as you trust in him, so that you may overflow with hope by the power of the Holy Spirit.

ROMANS 15:13

We continually remember before our God and Father your work produced by faith, your labor prompted by love, and your endurance inspired by hope in our Lord Jesus Christ.

1 THESSALONIANS 1:3

May our Lord Jesus Christ himself and God our Father, who loved us and by his grace gave us eternal encouragement and good hope, encourage your hearts and strengthen you in every good deed and word.

2 Thessalonians 2:16–17

We have God's hope as an anchor for the soul, firm and secure.

Hebrews 6:19

Now faith is being sure of what we hope for and certain of what we do not see.

Hebrews 11:1

In your hearts set apart Christ as Lord. Always be prepared to give an answer to everyone who asks you to give the reason for the hope that you have.

1 Peter 3:15

Though he slay me, yet will I hope in him. I will surely defend my ways to his face.

Job 13:15

Therefore my heart is glad and my tongue rejoices; my body also will live in hope, because you will not abandon me to the grave, nor will you let your Holy One see decay. You have made known to me the paths of life; you will fill me with joy in your presence.

ACTS 2:26–28

Be joyful in hope, patient in affliction, faithful in prayer.

ROMANS 12:12

DEVOTIONAL THOUGHT ON HOPE

All acts of hope expose themselves to ridicule because they seem impractical, failing to conform to visible reality. But in fact they are the reality that is being constructed but is not yet visible. Hope commits us to actions that connect with God's promises.

What we call hoping is often only wishing. We want things we think are impossible, but we have better sense than to spend any money or commit our lives to them.

Biblical hope, though, is an act. Hope acts on the conviction that God will complete the work that he has begun even when the appearances, especially when the appearances, oppose it.

Hope-determined actions participate in the future that God is bringing into being. These acts are rarely spectacular. Usually they take place outside sacred settings. Almost never are they perceived to be significant by bystanders.

It is not easy to act in hope because most of the immediate evidence is against it. It takes courage to act in hope. But it is the only practical action that survives the decay of the moment.

Eugene H. Peterson

GOD'S WORDS OF LIFE ON INTEGRITY

But if anyone obeys his word, God's love is truly made complete in him. This is how we know we are in him.

1 JOHN 2:5

Then the LORD said to Satan, "Have you considered my servant Job? There is no one on earth like him; he is blameless and upright, a man who fears God and shuns evil. And he still maintains his integrity, though you incited me against him to ruin him without any reason."

JOB 2:3

And Job Said, "I will never admit you are in the right; till I die, I will not deny my integrity."

JOB 27:5

May integrity and uprightness protect me,
because my hope is in you.

PSALM 25:21

Righteousness guards the man of integrity,
but wickedness overthrows the sinner.

PROVERBS 13:6

I put in charge of Jerusalem my brother Hanani, along with Hananiah the commander of the citadel, because he was a man of integrity and feared God more than most men do.

NEHEMIAH 7:2

He who walks righteously
and speaks what is right,
who rejects gain from extortion
and keeps his hand from accepting bribes,
who stops his ears against plots of murder
and shuts his eyes against contemplating evil—
this is the man who will dwell on the heights,
whose refuge will be the mountain fortress.
His bread will be supplied,
and water will not fail him.

ISAIAH 33:15–16

So in everything, do to others what you would have them do to you, for this sums up the Law and the Prophets.

MATTHEW 7:12

I strive always to keep my conscience clear before God and man.

ACTS 24:16

For we are taking pains to do what is right, not only in the eyes of the Lord but also in the eyes of men.

2 CORINTHIANS 8:21

Finally, brothers, whatever is true, whatever is noble, whatever is right, whatever is pure, whatever is lovely, whatever is admirable—if anything is excellent or praiseworthy—think about such things.

PHILIPPIANS 4:8

Pray for us. We are sure that we have a clear conscience and desire to live honorably in every way.

HEBREWS 13:18

Slaves, obey your earthly masters in everything; and do it, not only when their eye is on you and to win their favor, but with sincerity of heart and reverence for the Lord. Whatever you do, work at it with all your heart, as working for the Lord, not for men.

COLOSSIANS 3:22–23

Make it your ambition to lead a quiet life, to mind your own business and to work with your hands, just as we told you, so that your daily life may win the respect of outsiders and so that you will not be dependent on anybody.

1 Thessalonians 4:11–12

Live such good lives among the pagans that, though they accuse you of doing wrong, they may see your good deeds and glorify God on the day he visits us.

1 Peter 2:12

But select capable men from all the people—men who fear God, trustworthy men who hate dishonest gain.

Exodus 18:21

In everything set them an example by doing what is good. In your teaching show integrity, seriousness and soundness of speech that cannot be condemned, so that those who oppose you may be ashamed because they have nothing bad to say about us.

Titus 2:7–8

Let the Lord judge the peoples.
Judge me, O Lord, according to my righteousness,
according to my integrity, O Most High.

PSALM 7:8

Lord, who may dwell in your sanctuary?
Who may live on your holy hill?
He whose walk is blameless
and who does what is righteous,
who speaks the truth from his heart.

PSALM 15:1–2

Do not pervert justice or show partiality. Do not accept a bribe, for a bribe blinds the eyes of the wise and twists the words of the righteous. Follow justice and justice alone, so that you may live and possess the land the Lord your God is giving you.

DEUTERONOMY 16:19–20

The man of integrity walks securely,
but he who takes crooked paths will be found out.

PROVERBS 10:9

The integrity of the upright guides them,
but the unfaithful are destroyed by their
duplicity.

PROVERBS 11:3

He has showed you, O man, what is good.
And what does the LORD require of you?
To act justly and to love mercy
and to walk humbly with your God.

MICAH 6:8

Whoever can be trusted with very little can also be trusted with much, and whoever is dishonest with very little will also be dishonest with much.

LUKE 16:10

I know, my God, that you test the heart and are pleased with integrity. All these things have I given willingly and with honest intent.

1 CHRONICLES 29:17

DEVOTIONAL THOUGHT ON INTEGRITY

A father has to be careful of his promises, because a real man will follow through.

A real man is a man of integrity. That means going all out in everything he does. When he says something, you can count on it, take it to the bank. If I say I'm going to do something, you can consider it done. The first time I violate that, my credibility is shot. Our reputations are only as good as our last performances.

Unless the real men of this country—and there aren't many left—come together and align themselves under God, we're headed for catastrophe. God is looking for men who will obey and be what he wants them to be.

Mike Singletary

Do not seek revenge or bear a grudge against one of your people, but love your neighbor as yourself. I am the LORD.

LEVITICUS 19:18

Jesus said, "My command is this: Love each other as I have loved you. Greater love has no one than this, that he lay down his life for his friends."

JOHN 15:12–13

Be devoted to one another in brotherly love. Honor one another above yourselves.

ROMANS 12:10

You, my brothers, were called to be free. But do not use your freedom to indulge the sinful nature; rather, serve one another in love. The entire law is summed up in a single command: "Love your neighbor as yourself."

GALATIANS 5:13–14

How good and pleasant it is
when brothers live together in unity!

PSALM 133:1

Therefore, as we have opportunity, let us do good to all people, especially to those who belong to the family of believers.

GALATIANS 6:10

Live a life of love, just as Christ loved us and gave himself up for us as a fragrant offering and sacrifice to God.

EPHESIANS 5:2

May the Lord make your love increase and overflow for each other and for everyone else, just as ours does for you.

1 THESSALONIANS 3:12

Now about brotherly love we do not need to write to you, for you yourselves have been taught by God to love each other.

1 THESSALONIANS 4:9

Keep on loving each other as brothers.

HEBREWS 13:1

If you really keep the royal law found in Scripture, "Love your neighbor as yourself," you are doing right.

JAMES 2:8

Hatred stirs up dissension,
but love covers over all wrongs.

PROVERBS 10:12

Finally, all of you, live in harmony with one another; be sympathetic, love as brothers, be compassionate and humble. Do not repay evil with evil or insult with insult, but with blessing, because to this you were called so that you may inherit a blessing.

1 PETER 3:8–9

A new command I give you: Love one another. As I have loved you, so you must love one another. By this all men will know that you are my disciples, if you love one another.

JOHN 13:34–35

Now that you have purified yourselves by obeying the truth so that you have sincere love for your brothers, love one another deeply, from the heart.

1 PETER 1:22

Dear friends, let us love one another, for love comes from God. Everyone who loves has been born of God and knows God. Whoever does not love does not know God, because God is love.

1 JOHN 4:7–8

And he has given us this command: Whoever loves God must also love his brother.

1 JOHN 4:21

If I speak in the tongues of men and of angels, but have not love, I am only a resounding gong or a clanging cymbal. If I have the gift of prophecy and can fathom all mysteries and all knowledge, and if I have a faith that can move mountains, but have not love, I am nothing. If I give all I possess to the poor and surrender my body to the flames, but have not love, I gain nothing. Love is patient, love is kind. It does not envy, it does not boast, it is not proud. It is not rude, it is not self-seeking, it is not easily angered, it keeps no record of wrongs. Love does not delight in evil but rejoices with the truth. It always protects, always trusts, always hopes, always perseveres. Love never fails.

1 CORINTHIANS 13:1–8

No one has ever seen God; but if we love one another, God lives in us and his love is made complete in us.

1 JOHN 4:12

For in Christ Jesus neither circumcision nor uncircumcision has any value. The only thing that counts is faith expressing itself through love.

GALATIANS 5:6

But the fruit of the Spirit is love, joy, peace, patience, kindness, goodness, faithfulness.

GALATIANS 5:22

For God did not give us a spirit of timidity, but a spirit of power, of love and of self-discipline.

2 TIMOTHY 1:7

For God so loved the world that he gave his one and only Son, that whoever believes in him shall not perish but have eternal life.

JOHN 3:16

Above all, love each other deeply, because love covers over a multitude of sins.

1 PETER 4:8

And now these three remain: faith, hope and love. But the greatest of these is love.

1 CORINTHIANS 13:13

Jesus replied: "'Love the Lord your God with all your heart and with all your soul and with all your mind.' This is the first and greatest commandment. And the second is like it: 'Love your neighbor as yourself.' All the Law and the Prophets hang on these two commandments."

MATTHEW 22:37–40

DEVOTIONAL THOUGHT ON LOVE

When Jesus was asked to name the great commandments in the Scriptures, he didn't hesitate in the least. He told a young lawyer, "Love the Lord your God with all your heart and with all your soul and with all your mind. Love your neighbor as yourself" (Matthew 22:37, 39). Loving God, loving others and finding value in ourselves. Without a doubt, these three aspects of love are the most effective weapons against the destructive power of low self-worth.

Genuine love is a gift we give others. It isn't purchased by their actions or contingent upon our emotions at the moment. It may carry with it strong emotional feelings, but it isn't supported by them. Rather, it is a decision we make on a daily basis that someone is special and valuable to us. In fact, love for someone often begins to flow once we have made the decision to honor them.

Gary Smalley and John Trent

He has showed you, O man, what is good.
And what does the LORD *require of you?*
To act justly and to love mercy
and to walk humbly with your God.

MICAH 6:8

Blessed are the merciful, for they will be shown mercy.

MATTHEW 5:7

Be merciful, just as your Father is merciful.

LUKE 6:36

Judgment without mercy will be shown to anyone who has not been merciful. Mercy triumphs over judgment!

JAMES 2:13

And the LORD said, ". . . I will have mercy on whom I will have mercy, and I will have compassion on whom I will have compassion."

EXODUS 33:19

Praise be to the LORD,
for he has heard my cry for mercy.

PSALM 28:6

Let the wicked forsake his way
and the evil man his thoughts.
Let him turn to the LORD, and he will have mercy
on him,
and to our God, for he will freely pardon.

ISAIAH 55:7

Do not withhold your mercy from me, O LORD;
may your love and your truth always protect me.

PSALM 40:11

Answer me, O LORD, out of the goodness of your love;
in your great mercy turn to me.

PSALM 69:16

In all their distress [God] too was distressed,
and the angel of his presence saved them.
In his love and mercy he redeemed them;
he lifted them up and carried them
all the days of old.

ISAIAH 63:9

O LORD, hear my prayer,
listen to my cry for mercy;
in your faithfulness and righteousness
come to my relief.

PSALM 143:1

For I desire mercy, not sacrifice,
and acknowledgment of God rather than burnt
offerings.

HOSEA 6:6

Who is a God like you,
who pardons sin and forgives the transgression
of the remnant of his inheritance?
You do not stay angry forever
but delight to show mercy.

MICAH 7:18

This is what the Lord Almighty says: "Administer true justice; show mercy and compassion to one another."

ZECHARIAH 7:9

He who conceals his sins does not prosper,
*   but whoever confesses and renounces them finds*
*   mercy.*

PROVERBS 28:13

For he says to Moses, "I will have mercy on whom I have mercy, and I will have compassion on whom I have compassion." It does not, therefore, depend on man's desire or effort, but on God's mercy.

ROMANS 9:15–16

His mercy extends to those who fear him, from generation to generation.

LUKE 1:50

If it is encouraging, let him encourage; if it is contributing to the needs of others, let him give generously; if it is leadership, let him govern diligently; if it is showing mercy, let him do it cheerfully.

ROMANS 12:8

I urge you, brothers, in view of God's mercy, to offer your bodies as living sacrifices, holy and pleasing to God—this is your spiritual act of worship.

ROMANS 12:1

Let us then approach the throne of grace with confidence, so that we may receive mercy and find grace to help us in our time of need.

HEBREWS 4:16

But because of his great love for us, God, who is rich in mercy, made us alive with Christ even when we were dead in transgressions—it is by grace you have been saved.

EPHESIANS 2:4–5

David said to Gad, "I am in deep distress. Let me fall into the hands of the LORD, for his mercy is very great; but do not let me fall into the hands of men."

1 CHRONICLES 21:13

Mercy, peace and love be yours in abundance.

JUDE V. 2

The wisdom that comes from heaven is first of all pure; then peace-loving, considerate, submissive, full of mercy and good fruit, impartial and sincere.

JAMES 3:17

At one time we too were foolish, disobedient, deceived and enslaved by all kinds of passions and pleasures. We lived in malice and envy, being hated and hating one another. But when the kindness and love of God our Savior appeared, he saved us, not because of righteous things we had done, but because of his mercy.

TITUS 3:3–5

I knew that you are a gracious and compassionate God, slow to anger and abounding in love, a God who relents from sending calamity.

JONAH 4:2

DEVOTIONAL THOUGHT ON MERCY

Nothing expresses God's yearning to forgive better than the Book of Jonah. It contains but one line of prophecy: "Forty more days and Nineveh will be overturned" (3:4). But, to Jonah's disgust, that simple announcement of doom sparked a spiritual revival in hated Nineveh and changed God's plans for punishment.

Jonah, sulking under a shriveled vine, admitted he had suspected God's soft heart all along. Thus the whole madcap scenario of balky prophet, ocean storm, and whale detour came about because Jonah could not trust God—could not, that is, trust him to be harsh and unrelenting toward Nineveh.

As Robert Frost summed up the story, "After Jonah, you could never trust God not to be merciful again."

Philip Yancey

GOD'S WORDS OF LIFE ON
PEACE

You will keep in perfect peace him
whose mind is steadfast,
because he trusts in you.

ISAIAH 26:3

For [Jesus] himself is our peace, who has made the two one
and has destroyed the barrier, the dividing wall of hostility.

EPHESIANS 2:14

LORD, *you establish peace for us;*
all that we have accomplished you have done
for us.

ISAIAH 26:12

Whatever you have learned or received or heard from me,
or seen in me—put it into practice. And the God of peace
will be with you.

PHILIPPIANS 4:9

Let the peace of Christ rule in your hearts, since as members of one body you were called to peace. And be thankful.

COLOSSIANS 3:15

Do not be anxious about anything, but in everything, by prayer and petition, with thanksgiving, present your requests to God. And the peace of God, which transcends all understanding, will guard your hearts and your minds in Christ Jesus.

PHILIPPIANS 4:6–7

There will be trouble and distress for every human being who does evil . . . but glory, honor and peace for everyone who does good.

ROMANS 2:9–10

I will lie down and sleep in peace,
for you alone, O LORD,
make me dwell in safety.

PSALM 4:8

Jesus said, "Peace I leave with you; my peace I give you. I do not give to you as the world gives. Do not let your hearts be troubled and do not be afraid."

JOHN 14:27

*The L*ORD *gives strength to his people;*
*the L*ORD *blesses his people with peace.*

PSALM 29:11

Turn from evil and do good;
seek peace and pursue it.

PSALM 34:14

A heart at peace gives life to the body,
but envy rots the bones.

PROVERBS 14:30

But the meek will inherit the land
and enjoy great peace.

PSALM 37:11

Great peace have they who love your law,
and nothing can make them stumble.

PSALM 119:165

But the fruit of the Spirit is love, joy, peace, patience, kindness, goodness, faithfulness.

GALATIANS 5:22

Finally, brothers . . . aim for perfection, listen to my appeal, be of one mind, live in peace. And the God of love and peace will be with you.

2 CORINTHIANS 13:11

Make every effort to keep the unity of the Spirit through the bond of peace.

EPHESIANS 4:3

If it is possible, as far as it depends on you, live at peace with everyone.

ROMANS 12:18

But the wisdom that comes from heaven is first of all pure; then peace-loving, considerate, submissive, full of mercy and good fruit, impartial and sincere. Peacemakers who sow in peace raise a harvest of righteousness.

JAMES 3:17–18

When a man's ways are pleasing to the LORD,
* he makes even his enemies live at peace with him.*

PROVERBS 16:7

Let us therefore make very effort to do what leads to peace and to mutual edification.

ROMANS 14:19

Submit to God and be at peace with him;
in this way prosperity will come to you.

JOB 22:21

Consider the blameless, observe the upright;
there is a future for the man of peace.

PSALM 37:37

Discipline your son, and he will give you peace;
he will bring delight to your soul.

PROVERBS 29:17

The fruit of righteousness will be peace;
the effect of righteousness will be quietness and
confidence forever.

ISAIAH 32:17

Those who walk uprightly enter into peace;
they find rest as they lie in death.

ISAIAH 57:2

"Do not be afraid, O man highly esteemed," he said. "Peace! Be strong now; be strong."

DANIEL 10:19

Be at peace with each other.

MARK 9:50

Jesus said, "I have told you these things, so that in me you may have peace. In this world you will have trouble. But take heart! I have overcome the world."

JOHN 16:33

The mind of sinful man is death, but the mind controlled by the Spirit is life and peace.

ROMANS 8:6

Let us therefore make every effort to do what leads to peace and to mutual edification.

ROMANS 14:19

DEVOTIONAL THOUGHT ON PEACE

I had a tiny taste of success and a tiny taste of religion—but not much Christianity. Sure, I was a good person. I treated others with respect.

But someone once described the contrast between a good life and a godly life as the difference between the top of the ocean and the bottom. On top, sometimes it's like glass—serene and calm—and other times it's raging and stormy. But hundreds of fathoms below, it is beautiful and consistent, always calm, always peaceful.

Down deep in my heart, I did not have the peace that comes only from knowing Jesus Christ as a personal Savior. Back then in 1970, when I was twenty-nine years old and a head football coach for the first time in my life, I was a church-goer and a professing Christian. But it wasn't until four years later, when I was a rookie assistant coach at the University of Michigan, that I discovered a real relationship with Jesus Christ. And when I accepted Christ as Savior and Lord of my life, I began an adventure that has transformed my life.

Bill McCartney

GOD'S WORDS OF LIFE ON
POWER

Jesus looked at them and said, "With man this is impossible, but with God all things are possible."

MATTHEW 19:26

I am the LORD, the God of all mankind. Is anything too hard for me?

JEREMIAH 32:27

The LORD is slow to anger and great in power;
the LORD will not leave the guilty unpunished.
His way is in the whirlwind and the storm,
and clouds are the dust of his feet.

NAHUM 1:3

See now that I myself am He! There is no god besides me. I put to death and I bring to life, I have wounded and I will heal, and no one can deliver out of my hand.

DEUTERONOMY 32:39

All the peoples of the earth are regarded as nothing. God does as he pleases with the powers of heaven and the peoples of the earth. No one can hold back his hand or say to him: "What have you done?"

DANIEL 4:35

Wealth and honor come from you; you are the ruler of all things. In your hands are strength and power to exalt and give strength to all. Now, our God, we give you thanks, and praise your glorious name.

1 CHRONICLES 29:12–13

You are awesome, O God, in your sanctuary;
   the God of Israel gives power and strength to his
   people.
Praise be to God!

PSALM 68:35

But I have raised you up for this very purpose, that I might show you my power and that my name might be proclaimed in all the earth.

EXODUS 9:16

Being strengthened with all power according to his glorious might so that you may have great endurance and patience.

COLOSSIANS 1:11

To God belong wisdom and power;
counsel and understanding are his.

JOB 12:13

[God's] wisdom is profound, his power is vast.
Who has resisted him and come out unscathed?

JOB 9:4

Great is our LORD and mighty in power;
his understanding has no limit.

PSALM 147:5

A wise man has great power,
and a man of knowledge increases strength.

PROVERBS 24:5

Finally, be strong in the Lord and in his mighty power.

EPHESIANS 6:10

Yours, O LORD, is the greatness and the power and the glory and the majesty and the splendor, for everything in heaven and earth is yours. Yours, O LORD, is the kingdom; you are exalted as head over all. Wealth and honor come from you; you are the ruler of all things. In your hands are strength and power to exalt and give strength to all.

1 CHRONICLES 29:11–12

"This is the word of the LORD to Zerubbabel: 'Not by might nor by power, but by my Spirit,' says the LORD Almighty."

ZECHARIAH 4:6

You may say to yourself, "My power and the strength of my hands have produced this wealth for me." But remember the LORD your God, for it is he who gives you the ability to produce wealth, and so confirms his covenant, which he swore to your forefathers, as it is today.

DEUTERONOMY 8:17–18

DEVOTIONAL THOUGHT ON POWER

What makes the temptation of power so seemingly irresistible?

Maybe it is that power offers an easy substitute for the hard task of love. It seems easier to be God than to love God, easier to control people than to love people, easier to own life than to love life.

The long painful history of the church is the history of people ever and again tempted to choose power over love, control over the cross, being a leader over being led.

Those who resisted this temptation to the end and thereby give us hope are the true saints.

Henri Nouwen

GOD'S WORDS OF LIFE ON
PRAYER

LORD'S PRAYER   MATTHEW 6: 9-13
            Luke   11 : 2-4

Before they call I will answer;
while they are still speaking I will hear.

ISAIAH 65:24

Therefore I tell you, whatever you ask for in prayer, believe that you have received it, and it will be yours.

MARK 11:24

Ask and it will be given to you; seek and you will find; knock and the door will be opened to you. For everyone who asks receives; he who seeks finds; and to him who knocks, the door will be opened.

MATTHEW 7:7–8

Jesus said, "If you believe, you will receive whatever you ask for in prayer."

MATTHEW 21:22

Again, I tell you that if two of you on earth agree about anything you ask for, it will be done for you by my Father in heaven. For where two or three come together in my name, there am I with them.

MATTHEW 18:19–20

Dear friends, if our hearts do not condemn us, we have confidence before God and receive from him anything we ask, because we obey his commands and do what pleases him.

1 JOHN 3:21–22

The LORD is near to all who call on him,
to all who call on him in truth.

PSALM 145:18

Jesus answered, "In that day you will no longer ask me anything. I tell you the truth, my Father will give you whatever you ask in my name. Until now you have not asked for anything in my name. Ask and you will receive, and your joy will be complete."

JOHN 16:23–24

But when you pray, go into your room, close the door and pray to your Father, who is unseen. Then your Father, who sees what is done in secret, will reward you.

MATTHEW 6:6

Call to me and I will answer you and tell you great and unsearchable things you do not know.

JEREMIAH 33:3

He will call upon me, and I will answer him;
   I will be with him in trouble,
   I will deliver him and honor him.

PSALM 91:15

The LORD is far from the wicked
   but he hears the prayer of the righteous.

PROVERBS 15:29

Delight yourself in the LORD
   and he will give you the desires of your heart.

PSALM 37:4

If you remain in me and my words remain in you, ask whatever you wish, and it will be given you.

JOHN 15:7

And I will do whatever you ask in my name, so that the Son may bring glory to the Father. You may ask me for anything in my name, and I will do it.

JOHN 14:13–14

I wait for you, O LORD;
you will answer, O LORD my God.

PSALM 38:15

If we confess our sins, he is faithful and just and will forgive us our sins and purify us from all unrighteousness.

1 JOHN 1:9

Very early in the morning, while it was still dark, Jesus got up, left the house and went off to a solitary place, where he prayed.

MARK 1:35

And when you pray, do not be like the hypocrites, for they love to pray standing in the synagogues and on the street corners to be seen by men. I tell you the truth, they have received their reward in full.

MATTHEW 6:5

Do not be anxious about anything, but in everything, by prayer and petition, with thanksgiving, present your requests to God. And the peace of God, which transcends all understanding, will guard your hearts and your minds in Christ Jesus.

PHILIPPIANS 4:6–7

Is any one of you in trouble? He should pray. Is anyone happy? Let him sing songs of praise. Is any one of you sick? He should call the elders of the church to pray over him and anoint him with oil in the name of the Lord. And the prayer offered in faith will make the sick person well; the Lord will raise him up. If he has sinned, he will be forgiven. Therefore confess your sins to each other and pray for each other so that you may be healed. The prayer of a righteous man is powerful and effective.

JAMES 5:13–16

This is the confidence we have in approaching God: that if we ask anything according to his will, he hears us. And if we know that he hears us—whatever we ask—we know that we have what we asked of him.

1 JOHN 5:14–15

For the eyes of the Lord are on the righteous and his ears are attentive to their prayer.

1 PETER 3:12

Let us then approach the throne of grace with confidence, so that we may receive mercy and find grace to help us in our time of need.

HEBREWS 4:16

If my people, who are called by my name, will humble themselves and pray and seek my face and turn from their wicked ways, then will I hear from heaven and will forgive their sin and will heal their land.

2 CHRONICLES 7:14

Out of the depths I cry to you, O LORD;
O LORD, hear my voice.
Let your ears be attentive
to my cry for mercy.

PSALM 130:1–2

DEVOTIONAL THOUGHT ON PRAYER

The Biblical Christian can only pray empty-handed, as the thirteenth-century Dominican preacher William Peraldus expressed it. Our hope depends not on the right technique or the proper phrase or gesture, which borders on magic, but on the promises of God.

As I see it, true prayer is neither mystical rapture nor ritual observance nor philosophical reflection: it is the out-pouring of the soul before a living God, the crying to God "out of the depths." Such prayer can only be uttered by one convicted of sin by the grace of God and moved to confession by the Spirit of God.

True prayer is an encounter with the Holy in which we realize not only our creatureliness and guilt but also the joy of knowing that our sins are forgiven through the atoning death of the divine Savior, Jesus Christ. In such an encounter, we are impelled not only to bow before God and seek his mercy but also to offer thanksgiving for grace that goes out to undeserving sinners.

Donald Bloesch

GOD'S WORDS OF LIFE ON
PRIDE

To fear the LORD is to hate evil;
I hate pride and arrogance,
evil behavior and perverse speech.

PROVERBS 8:13

Pride only breeds quarrels,
but wisdom is found in those who take advice.

PROVERBS 13:10

When pride comes, then comes disgrace,
but with humility comes wisdom.

PROVERBS 11:2

A man's pride brings him low,
but a man of lowly spirit gains honor.

PROVERBS 29:23

Everyone who exalts himself will be humbled, and he who humbles himself will be exalted.

Luke 18:14

For by the grace given me I say to every one of you: Do not think of yourself more highly than you ought, but rather think of yourself with sober judgment, in accordance with the measure of faith God has given you.

Romans 12:3

The eyes of the arrogant man will be humbled
and the pride of men brought low;
the LORD alone will be exalted in that day.

Isaiah 2:11

DEVOTIONAL THOUGHT ON PRIDE

When some people begin to experience a degree of success, they become overly confident of their own abilities. They behave as if no one else in the world can do what they do. That is to say, they get an exaggerated sense of their own importance and are puffed up with pride, making it difficult for most people to work with them.

These swollen-headed types also usually cease learning. Why shouldn't they? Don't they already know everything in their field (or assume they do)? Despite their talent, they lose their usefulness. They tend to do little but think about themselves. Instead of singing the hymn "How Great Thou Art," their words sound like "How Great I Am." I have worked out a simple formula for humility.

IF WE RECOGNIZE THAT:

God created this universe, including us, and God shows that he is much more powerful than we are by what he does and has done in our world, and God gives each of us abilities that we cannot supply to ourselves or explain our worthiness of, THEN WE ARE HUMBLED.

Ben Carson

GOD'S WORDS OF LIFE ON
RELATIONSHIPS

Bear with each other and forgive whatever grievances you may have against one another. Forgive as the Lord forgave you.

COLOSSIANS 3:13

Be completely humble and gentle; be patient, bearing with one another in love. Make every effort to keep the unity of the Spirit through the bond of peace.

EPHESIANS 4:2–3

Two are better than one, because they have a good return for their work: If one falls down, his friend can help him up. But pity the man who falls and has no one to help him up! . . . Though one may be overpowered, two can defend themselves. A cord of three strands is not quickly broken.

ECCLESIASTES 4:9–12

Do not be yoked together with unbelievers. For what do righteousness and wickedness have in common? Or what fellowship can light have with darkness? . . . What does a believer have in common with an unbeliever? . . . For we are the temple of the living God. As God has said: "I will live with them and walk among them, and I will be their God, and they will be my people." Therefore come out from them and be separate, says the Lord."

2 CORINTHIANS 6:14–17

For by the grace given me I say to every one of you: Do not think of yourself more highly than you ought, but rather think of yourself with sober judgment, in accordance with the measure of faith God has given you. Just as each of us has one body with many members, and these members do not all have the same function, so in Christ we who are many form one body, and each member belongs to all the others.

ROMANS 12:3–5

In everything set them an example by doing what is good. In your teaching show integrity, seriousness and soundness of speech that cannot be condemned, so that those who oppose you may be ashamed because they have nothing bad to say about us.

TITUS 2:7–8

As iron sharpens iron,
so one man sharpens another.

Proverbs 27:17

Then Peter began to speak: "I now realize how true it is that God does not show favoritism but accepts men from every nation who fear him and do what is right."

Acts 10:34–35

The Lord does not look at the things man looks at. Man looks at the outward appearance, but the Lord looks at the heart.

1 Samuel 16:7

My brothers, as believers in our glorious Lord Jesus Christ, don't show favoritism.

James 2:1

See that you do not look down on one of these little ones. For I tell you that their angels in heaven always see the face of my Father in heaven.

Matthew 18:10

Love one another deeply, from the heart.

1 Peter 1:22

Do not rebuke an older man harshly, but exhort him as if he were your father. Treat younger men as brothers, older women as mothers, and younger women as sisters, with absolute purity.

1 TIMOTHY 5:1–2

 Carry each other's burdens, and in this way you will fulfill the law of Christ.

GALATIANS 6:2

Give everyone what you owe him: If you owe taxes, pay taxes; if revenue, then revenue; if respect, then respect; if honor, then honor. Let no debt remain outstanding, except the continuing debt to love one another.

ROMANS 13:7–8

Peacemakers who sow in peace raise a harvest of righteousness.

JAMES 3:18

All of you, clothe yourselves with humility toward one another, because, "God opposes the proud but gives grace to the humble." Humble yourselves, therefore, under God's mighty hand, that he may lift you up.

1 PETER 5:5– 6

Whoever wants to become great among you must be your servant, and whoever wants to be first must be your slave—just as the Son of Man did not come to be served, but to serve, and to give his life as a ransom for many.

MATTHEW 20:26–28

And the Lord's servant must not quarrel; instead, he must be kind to everyone, able to teach, not resentful. Those who oppose him he must gently instruct, in the hope that God will grant them repentance leading them to a knowledge of the truth.

2 TIMOTHY 2:24–25

A man's wisdom gives him patience;
it is to his glory to overlook an offense.
PROVERBS 19:11

I appeal to you, brothers, in the name of our Lord Jesus Christ, that all of you agree with one another so that there may be no divisions among you and that you may be perfectly united in mind and thought.

1 CORINTHIANS 1:10

Jesus said, "Why do you look at the speck of sawdust in your brother's eye and pay no attention to the plank in your own eye? How can you say to your brother, 'Brother, let me take the speck out of your eye,' when you yourself fail to see the plank in your own eye? You hypocrite, first take the plank out of your eye, and then you will see clearly to remove the speck from your brother's eye."

LUKE 6:41–42

Let the peace of Christ rule in your hearts, since as members of one body you were called to peace. And be thankful. Let the word of Christ dwell in you richly as you teach and admonish one another with all wisdom, and as you sing psalms, hymns and spiritual songs with gratitude in your hearts to God. And whatever you do, whether in word or deed, do it all in the name of the Lord Jesus, giving thanks to God the Father through him.

COLOSSIANS 3:15–17

DEVOTIONAL THOUGHT ON RELATIONSHIPS

You get what you give out. You want a loving God? Then be loving. You want a merciful God? Then be merciful. Want God to forgive you? Then forgive your fellowman. Want God to condemn you? Then be an accusatory person. Want to put yourself above the rest of the world? Then get ready for a God who is going to strain out every judgmental thought you've ever had and measure all the thoughts and intents of your hidden heart by the same standard.

You and I as Christians need to realize that however acceptable our lives may be for the general audience, we still possess an R-rated heart, and we're as good as dead if we want God to meet us on any other ground than his grace and forgiveness.

The joy of this truth is that once I can believe that forgiveness for myself, then I can believe it for anybody. I have new eyes to see beyond my neighbor's sin and love him or her with the love of Christ.

John Fischer

GOD'S WORDS OF LIFE ON
RIGHTEOUS LIVING

Love the LORD your God with all your heart and with all your soul and with all your strength.

DEUTERONOMY 6:5

Be very careful to keep the commandment and the law that Moses the servant of the LORD gave you: to love the LORD your God, to walk in all his ways, to obey his commands, to hold fast to him and to serve him with all your heart and all your soul.

JOSHUA 22:5

Since, then, you have been raised with Christ, set your hearts on things above, where Christ is seated at the right hand of God. Set your minds on things above, not on earthly things.

COLOSSIANS 3:1–2

You desire truth in the inner parts;
you teach me wisdom in the inmost place.

PSALM 51:6

lessed is the man
    who does not walk in the counsel of the wicked
stand in the way of sinners
    or sit in the seat of mockers.
t his delight is in the law of the LORD,
    and on his law he meditates day and night.

PSALM 1:1–2

will keep in perfect peace
    him whose mind is steadfast,
    because he trusts in you.

ISAIAH 26:3

f sinful man is death, but the mind controlled
    is life and peace.

ROMANS 8:6

lom of God is not a matter of eating and drink-
ghteousness, peace and joy in the Holy Spirit.

ROMANS 14:17

Blessed are those who hunger and thirst for righteousness,
for they will be filled.

MATTHEW 5:6

Do not work for food that spoils, but for food that endures to eternal life, which the Son of Man will give you. On him God the Father has placed his seal of approval.

JOHN 6:27

Be careful that you do not forget the LORD your God, failing to observe his commands, his laws and his decrees that I am giving you this day. Otherwise, when you eat and are satisfied, when you build fine houses and settle down, and when your herds and flocks grow large and your silver and gold increase and all you have is multiplied, then your heart will become proud and you will forget the LORD your God.

DEUTERONOMY 8:11–14

Only be careful, and watch yourselves closely so that you do not forget the things your eyes have seen or let them slip from your heart as long as you live. Teach them to your children and to their children after them.

DEUTERONOMY 4:9

Being confident of this, that he who began a good work in you will carry it on to completion until the day of Christ Jesus.

PHILIPPIANS 1:6

*This is what the L*ORD *says:*
    "Stand at the crossroads and look;
ask for the ancient paths,
    ask where the good way is, and walk in it,
    and you will find rest for your souls."

JEREMIAH 6:16

Do your best to present yourself to God as one approved, a workman who does not need to be ashamed and who correctly handles the word of truth.

2 TIMOTHY 2:15

And this is my prayer: that your love may abound more and more in knowledge and depth of insight, so that you may be able to discern what is best and may be pure and blameless until the day of Christ.

PHILIPPIANS 1:9–10

DEVOTIONAL THOUGHT ON RIGHTEOUS LIVING

Very few believers choose to drift; seldom do Christians plan to be lukewarm. But poor performance undermines confidence and failure causes discouragement. Temptation, even when overcome, leaves us battle-scarred and weary. It is sometimes difficult to tell the difference between victory and defeat because issues are never clear-cut and our successes never total. When one has struggled through the testing time and finally endured, it seldom feels like triumph.

Someone has to help us at the time of our struggle. We need a brother in the hour of trial, and especially when we fail. Otherwise we fall into the discouragement of trying harder or of never quite measuring up. The subtle shift from trust in Christ to our own self-efforts robs us of hope and joy. We begin to tally hurts, count disappointments and weigh sacrifices. And already the drift has set in. We need the warning, but more than that, we need to know that we are known, understood and loved by someone who has marked out the path, has won the victory and is with us on the way. That someone is Jesus.

Reuben R. Welch

Listen, my sons, to a father's instruction;
pay attention and gain understanding.

PROVERBS 4:1

My son, keep my words
and store up my commands within you.
Keep my commands and you will live;
guard my teachings as the apple of your eye.
Bind them on your fingers;
write them on the tablet of your heart.

PROVERBS 7:1–3

Jesus said, "As for the person who hears my words but does not keep them, I do not judge him. For I did not come to judge the world, but to save it. There is a judge for the one who rejects me and does not accept my words; that very word which I spoke will condemn him at the last day."

JOHN 12:47–48

I wish that all men were as I am. But each man has his own gift from God.

1 CORINTHIANS 7:7

But when the kindness and love of God our Savior appeared, he saved us, not because of righteous things we had done, but because of his mercy. He saved us through the washing of rebirth and renewal by the Holy Spirit, whom he poured out on us generously through Jesus Christ our Savior, so that, having been justified by his grace, we might become heirs having the hope of eternal life. This is a trustworthy saying. And I want you to stress these things, so that those who have trusted in God may be careful to devote themselves to doing what is good. These things are excellent and profitable for everyone.

TITUS 3:4–8

To this you were called, because Christ suffered for you, leaving you an example, that you should follow in his steps.

1 PETER 2:21

Be imitators of God, therefore, as dearly loved children and live a life of love, just as Christ loved us and gave himself up for us as a fragrant offering and sacrifice to God.

EPHESIANS 5:1–2

Whoever wants to become great among you must be your servant, and whoever wants to be first must be slave of all.

MARK 10:43–44

Jesus said, "I have set you an example that you should do as I have done for you."

JOHN 13:15

This is how we know what love is: Jesus Christ laid down his life for us. And we ought to lay down our lives for our brothers.

1 JOHN 3:16

Dear children, let us not love with words or tongue but with actions and in truth.

1 JOHN 3:18

Don't let anyone look down on you because you are young, but set an example for the believers in speech, in life, in love, in faith and in purity.

1 TIMOTHY 4:12

In everything set them an example by doing what is good. In your teaching show integrity, seriousness and soundness of speech that cannot be condemned, so that those who oppose you may be ashamed because they have nothing bad to say about us.

TITUS 2:7–8

Be shepherds of God's flock that is under your care, serving as overseers—not because you must, but because you are willing, as God wants you to be; not greedy for money, but eager to serve; not lording it over those entrusted to you, but being examples to the flock.

1 PETER 5:2–3

[God] will turn the hearts of the fathers to their children, and the hearts of the children to their fathers.

MALACHI 4:6

DEVOTIONAL THOUGHT ON ROLE MODELS

Little boys are the hope of the next generation. They are the fathers of tomorrow. They must know who they are and what they are to do. They must see their role model in action. That's how they will know what it means to be a male. That puts the ball in my court . . . and in yours.

It's our job to save the boys. So the question is, how are we going to do that? I must have a pretty clear idea of what I need to teach them. I must ask myself: What do I specifically need to do in order to train them to become leaders of their families?

It is my job . . . to model for them the importance of . . .

knowing and obeying Jesus Christ,
knowing and displaying godly character,
knowing and loving my wife,
knowing and loving my children, and
knowing my gifts and abilities.

Then I can work hard and effectively in an area of strength, rather than weakness, and contribute effectively to the lives of others—and have a little fun at the same time.

Steve Farrar

GOD'S WORDS OF LIFE ON
SERVANTHOOD

The greatest among you will be your servant.

MATTHEW 23:11

Whoever wants to become great among you must be your servant, and whoever wants to be first must be slave of all.

MARK 10:43–44

Jesus said, "The greatest among you should be like the youngest, and the one who rules like the one who serves. For who is greater, the one who is at the table or the one who serves? Is it not the one who is at the table? But I am among you as one who serves."

LUKE 22:26–27

I have set you an example that you should do as I have done for you. I tell you the truth, no servant is greater than his master, nor is a messenger greater than the one who sent him.

JOHN 13:15–16

Though I am free and belong to no man, I make myself a slave to everyone, to win as many as possible. To the Jews I became like a Jew, to win the Jews. To those under the law I became like one under the law (though I myself am not under the law), so as to win those under the law. To those not having the law I became like one not having the law (though I am not free from God's law but am under Christ's law), so as to win those not having the law. To the weak I became weak, to win the weak. I have become all things to all men so that by all possible means I might save some.

1 CORINTHIANS 9:19–22

Your attitude should be the same as that of Christ Jesus: Who, being in very nature God, did not consider equality with God something to be grasped, but made himself nothing, taking the very nature of a servant, being made in human likeness. And being found in appearance as a man, he humbled himself and became obedient to death—even death on a cross!

PHILIPPIANS 2:5–8

There are different kinds of service, but the same Lord.

1 CORINTHIANS 12:5

But be very careful to keep the commandment and the law that Moses the servant of the LORD gave you: to love the LORD your God, to walk in all his ways, to obey his commands, to hold fast to him and to serve him with all your heart and all your soul.

JOSHUA 22:5

For whoever wants to save his life will lose it, but whoever loses his life for me will find it.

MATTHEW 16:25

It is the LORD your God you must follow, and him you must revere. Keep his commands and obey him; serve him and hold fast to him.

DEUTERONOMY 13:4

Worship the Lord your God, and serve him only.

MATTHEW 4:10

Be devoted to one another in brotherly love. Honor one another above yourselves. Never be lacking in zeal, but keep your spiritual fervor, serving the Lord.

ROMANS 12:10–11

But if serving the LORD seems undesirable to you, then choose for yourselves this day whom you will serve, whether the gods your forefathers served beyond the River, or the gods of the Amorites, in whose land you are living. But as for me and my household, we will serve the LORD.

JOSHUA 24:15

And now, O Israel, what does the LORD your God ask of you but to fear the LORD your God, to walk in all his ways, to love him, to serve the LORD your God with all your heart and with all your soul, and to observe the LORD's commands and decrees that I am giving you today for your own good.

DEUTERONOMY 10:12–13

Be sure to fear the LORD and serve him faithfully with all your heart; consider what great things he has done for you.

1 SAMUEL 12:24

Whoever wants to become great among you must be your servant, and whoever wants to be first must be your slave.

MATTHEW 20:26–27

Jesus said to them, "Whoever welcomes this little child in my name welcomes me; and whoever welcomes me welcomes the one who sent me. For he who is least among you all—he is the greatest."

LUKE 9:48

If anyone speaks, he should do it as one speaking the very words of God. If anyone serves, he should do it with the strength God provides, so that in all things God may be praised through Jesus Christ. To him be the glory and the power for ever and ever. Amen.

1 PETER 4:11

You, my brothers, were called to be free. But do not use your freedom to indulge the sinful nature, rather, serve one another in love.

GALATIANS 5:13

Sitting down, Jesus called the Twelve and said, "If anyone wants to be first, he must be the very last, and the servant of all."

MARK 9:35

Jesus said, "The man who loves his life will lose it, while the man who hates his life in this world will keep it for eternal life. Whoever serves me must follow me; and where I am, my servant also will be. My Father will honor the one who serves me."

JOHN 12:25–26

My command is this: Love each other as I have loved you. Greater love has no one than this, that he lay down his life for his friends. You are my friends if you do what I command. I no longer call you servants, because a servant does not know his master's business. Instead, I have called you friends, for everything that I learned from my Father I have made known to you. You did not choose me, but I chose you and appointed you to go and bear fruit—fruit that will last. Then the Father will give you whatever you ask in my name. This is my command: Love each other.

JOHN 15:12–17

DEVOTIONAL THOUGHT ON SERVANTHOOD

Leadership shared in mutual respect can establish a climate of dignity, freedom and responsibility, creating an atmosphere which is both comforting and stimulating . . . a Christian atmosphere.

But where one seizes power, or struggles for control, an atmosphere of competition and conflict chokes communication and understanding. Even the unconscious assuming of power will mold the relationship in ways neither desire.

Leadership is a function which should always be shared. Authority in one area or another is a responsibility which is mutually designated to one or the other through honest negotiation. It can be renegotiated at any time.

To be a man—is to possess the strength to love another, not the need to dominate over others.

To be a man—is to experience the courage to accept another, not the compulsion to be an aggressor.

To be a man—is to keep faith with human values in relationships, not to value oneself by position or possessions.

To be a man—is to be free to give love and to be free to accept love in return.

David Augsburger

GOD'S WORDS OF LIFE ON SEXUAL INTIMACY

Turn my eyes away from worthless things;
preserve my life according to your word.

PSALM 119:37

Let your eyes look straight ahead,
fix your gaze directly before you.
Make level paths for your feet
and take only ways that are firm.
Do not swerve to the right or the left;
keep your foot from evil.

PROVERBS 4:25–27

It is God's will that you should be sanctified: that you should avoid sexual immorality; that each of you should learn to control his own body in a way that is holy and honorable, not in passionate lust like the heathen, who do not know God. . . . For God did not call us to be impure, but to live a holy life.

1 THESSALONIANS 4:3–5, 7

Flee from sexual immorality. All other sins a man commits are outside his body, but he who sins sexually sins against his own body. Do you not know that your body is a temple of the Holy Spirit, who is in you, whom you have received from God? You are not your own; you were bought at a price. Therefore honor God with your body.

1 Corinthians 6:18–20

For everything in the world—the cravings of sinful man, the lust of his eyes and the boasting of what he has and does—comes not from the Father but from the world. The world and its desires pass away, but the man who does the will of God lives forever.

1 John 2:16–17

But each one is tempted when, by his own evil desire, he is dragged away and enticed. Then, after desire has conceived, it gives birth to sin; and sin, when it is full-grown, gives birth to death. Don't be deceived, my dear brothers.

James 1:14–16

A man's ways are in full view of the Lord,
and he examines all his paths.

Proverbs 5:21

Husbands ought to love their wives as their own bodies. He who loves his wife loves himself. After all, no one ever hated his own body, but he feeds and cares for it, just as Christ does the church.

EPHESIANS 5:28–29

No temptation has seized you except what is common to man. And God is faithful; he will not let you be tempted beyond what you can bear. But when you are tempted, he will also provide a way out so that you can stand up under it.

1 CORINTHIANS 10:13

But among you there must not be even a hint of sexual immorality, or of any kind of impurity, or of greed, because these are improper for God's holy people.

EPHESIANS 5:3

But since there is so much immorality, each man should have his own wife, and each woman her own husband. The husband should fulfill his marital duty to his wife, and likewise the wife to her husband. The wife's body does not belong to her alone but also to her husband. In the same way, the husband's body does not belong to him alone but also to his wife. Do not deprive each other except by mutual consent and for a time, so that you may devote yourselves to prayer. Then come together again so that Satan will not tempt you because of your lack of self-control.

1 Corinthians 7:2–5

I made a covenant with my eyes
not to look lustfully at a girl.

Job 31:1

DEVOTIONAL THOUGHT ON SEXUAL INTIMACY

A one-woman kind of man is a man who demonstrates his commitment by disciplining his eyes. We are all familiar with the guy who can't walk one block without giving some woman the once-over from head to toe. He will even stop dead in his tracks in the flow of pedestrian traffic to turn and watch her as she goes by. Most of us are a little better socially adjusted than that.

A man who is committed with his eyes will avoid certain kinds of magazines and television programs. A hotel room on the road can be a very dangerous place for a one-woman kind of man who is not prepared for battle. When I bought a newspaper this morning, it was surrounded by pornographic magazines with alluring covers. "Girls of the Southwest Conference!" blazed the cover. If I don't discipline my eyes and look away, I'm going to start wondering how those girls in the Southwest Conference are getting along. And I must particularly cultivate that blindness away from home. I know I must do this because I know myself. And the self I know has a hard enough time even when I'm not away from home.

Steve Farrar

GOD'S WORDS OF LIFE ON
STRENGTH

The LORD gives strength to his people;
the LORD blesses his people with peace.

PSALM 29:11

So do not fear, for I am with you;
do not be dismayed, for I am your God.
I will strengthen you and help you;
I will uphold you with my righteous right hand.

ISAIAH 41:10

But he said to me, "My grace is sufficient for you, for my power is made perfect in weakness." Therefore I will boast all the more gladly about my weaknesses, so that Christ's power may rest on me. That is why, for Christ's sake, I delight in weaknesses, in insults, in hardships, in persecutions, in difficulties. For when I am weak, then I am strong.

2 CORINTHIANS 12:9–10

I can do everything through him who gives me strength.

PHILIPPIANS 4:13

Being strengthened with all power according to his glorious might so that you may have great endurance and patience, and joyfully giving thanks to the Father, who has qualified you to share in the inheritance of the saints in the kingdom of light.

COLOSSIANS 1:11–12

The LORD is the strength of his people,
a fortress of salvation for his anointed one.

PSALM 28:8

In the LORD alone
are righteousness and strength.

ISAIAH 45:24

Be strong in the Lord and in his mighty power.

EPHESIANS 6:10

The righteous will hold to their ways,
and those with clean hands will grow stronger.

JOB 17:9

I pray that out of his glorious riches he may strengthen you
with power through his Spirit in your inner being, so that
Christ may dwell in your hearts through faith.

EPHESIANS 3:16–17

You are awesome, O God, in your sanctuary;
    the God of Israel gives power and strength to his
      people.
Praise be to God!

PSALM 68:35

But those who hope in the LORD
    will renew their strength.
They will soar on wings like eagles;
    they will run and not grow weary,
    they will walk and not be faint.

ISAIAH 40:31

"I will strengthen them in the LORD
    and in his name they will walk,"
    declares the LORD.

ZECHARIAH 10:12

Wealth and honor come from you; you are the ruler of all things. In your hands are strength and power to exalt and give strength to all.

1 CHRONICLES 29:12

Therefore we do not lose heart. Though outwardly we are wasting away, yet inwardly we are being renewed day by day.

2 CORINTHIANS 4:16

Therefore, since we are surrounded by such a great cloud of witnesses, let us throw off everything that hinders and the sin that so easily entangles, and let us run with perseverance the race marked out for us.

HEBREWS 12:1

My soul is weary with sorrow;
  strengthen me according to your word.

PSALM 119:28

He gives strength to the weary
  and increases the power of the weak.

ISAIAH 40:29

DEVOTIONAL THOUGHT ON STRENGTH

Whenever there is the experience of weariness or degradation, you may be certain you have done one of two things—either you have disregarded a law of nature, or you have deliberately got out of touch with God.

There is no such thing as weariness in God's work. If you are in tune with the joy of God, the more you spend out in God's service, the more the recuperation goes on, and when once the warning note of weariness is given, it is a sign that something has gone wrong. If only we would heed the warning, we would find it is God's wonderfully gentle way of saying—"Not that way; that must be left alone; this must be given up."

Spiritual fatigue comes from the unconscious frittering away of God's time. When you feel weary or are exhausted, don't ask for hot milk, but get back to God. The secret of weariness and nervous disease in the natural world is a lack of a dominating interest, and the same is true in spiritual life. It is Christian activity that counts . . . and every moment is filled with an energy that is not our own, a super-abounding life that nothing can stand before.

Oswald Chambers

Come to me, all you who are weary and burdened, and I will give you rest. Take my yoke upon you and learn from me, for I am gentle and humble in heart, and you will find rest for your souls. For my yoke is easy and my burden is light.

MATTHEW 11:28–30

This is what the Sovereign LORD, the Holy One of Israel, says:

"In repentance and rest is your salvation,
in quietness and trust is your strength,
but you would have none of it."

ISAIAH 30:15

You are awesome, O God, in your sanctuary;
the God of Israel gives power and strength to
his people.
Praise be to God!

PSALM 68:35

He gives strength to the weary
and increases the power of the weak.
Even youths grow tired and weary,
and young men stumble and fall;
but those who hope in the LORD
will renew their strength.
They will soar on wings like eagles;
they will run and not grow weary,
they will walk and not be faint.

ISAIAH 40:29–31

Remember the Sabbath day by keeping it holy. Six days you shall labor and do all your work, but the seventh day is a Sabbath to the LORD your God. On it you shall not do any work, neither you, nor your son or daughter, nor your manservant or maidservant, nor your animals, nor the alien within your gates. For in six days the LORD made the heavens and the earth, the sea, and all that is in them, but he rested on the seventh day. Therefore the LORD blessed the Sabbath day and made it holy.

EXODUS 20:8–11

Therefore, since the promise of entering his rest still stands, let us be careful that none of you be found to have fallen short of it.

HEBREWS 4:1

So do not fear, for I am with you;
  do not be dismayed, for I am your God.
I will strengthen you and help you;
  I will uphold you with my righteous right hand.

ISAIAH 41:10

I will refresh the weary and satisfy the faint.

JEREMIAH 31:25

Be strong in the Lord and in his mighty power.

EPHESIANS 6:10

Unless the LORD builds the house,
  its builders labor in vain.
Unless the LORD watches over the city,
  the watchmen stand guard in vain.
In vain you rise early
  and stay up late,
toiling for food to eat—
  for he grants sleep to those he loves.

PSALM 127:1–2

Let us not become weary in doing good, for at the proper time we will reap a harvest if we do not give up.

GALATIANS 6:9

He makes me lie down in green pastures,
he leads me beside quiet waters,
*   he restores my soul.*
He guides me in paths of righteousness
*   for his name's sake.*

PSALM 23:2–3

By the seventh day God had finished the work he had been doing; so on the seventh day he rested from all his work.

GENESIS 2:2

There remains, then, a Sabbath-rest for the people of God; for anyone who enters God's rest also rests from his own work, just as God did from his. Let us, therefore, make every effort to enter that rest, so that no one will fall by following their example of disobedience.

HEBREWS 4:9–11

Then, because so many people were coming and going that they did not even have a chance to eat, Jesus said to them, "Come with me by yourselves to a quiet place and get some rest."

MARK 6:31

DEVOTIONAL THOUGHT ON STRESS

Too much stress—especially stress that is not relieved by times of rest and renewal—can harm us physically, mentally and spiritually.

To a great extent Christians are caught up in the same rat race as everyone else. We have let our values become distorted and don't see life clearly from God's perspective. We've lost some of our distinctiveness; our lives are almost identical to those of people who are not committed to Christ. As a result, I believe we are violating very basic laws that God has set down for our bodies. And we may be doing all this in the name of the One who came to save us from our need to earn salvation!

Christians must wake up to the fact that they are burning themselves out just as quickly as everyone else is! Change is occurring so rapidly and hurry sickness is so rampant in our society that avoiding stress damage takes an extra effort. And the sad fact is that relatively few people—even Christians—are making that extra effort.

Archibald Hart

GOD'S WORDS OF LIFE ON
SUCCESS

Be strong and very courageous. Be careful to obey all the law my servant Moses gave you; do not turn from it to the right or to the left, that you may be successful wherever you go. Do not let this Book of the Law depart from your mouth; meditate on it day and night, so that you may be careful to do everything written in it. Then you will be prosperous and successful.

JOSHUA 1:7–8

Then you will have success if you are careful to observe the decrees and laws that the LORD gave Moses for Israel. Be strong and courageous. Do not be afraid or discouraged.

1 CHRONICLES 22:13

King Uzziah sought God during the days of Zechariah, who instructed him in the fear of God. As long as he sought the LORD, God gave him success.

2 CHRONICLES 26:5

Blessed is the man
    who does not walk in the counsel of the wicked
or stand in the way of sinners
    or sit in the seat of mockers.
But his delight is in the law of the LORD,
    and on his law he meditates day and night.
He is like a tree planted by streams of water,
    which yields its fruit in season
and whose leaf does not wither.
    Whatever he does prospers.

PSALM 1:1–3

"I am about to go the way of all the earth," David said. "So be strong, show yourself a man, and observe what the LORD your God requires: Walk in his ways, and keep his decrees and commands, his laws and requirements, so that you may prosper in all you do and wherever you go."

1 KINGS 2:2–3

In everything that he undertook in the service of God's temple and in obedience to the law and the commands, he sought his God and worked wholeheartedly. And so he prospered.

2 CHRONICLES 31:21

When his master saw that the LORD was with him and that the LORD gave him success in everything he did, Joseph found favor in his eyes and became his attendant. Potiphar put him in charge of his household, and he entrusted to his care everything he owned.

GENESIS 39:3–4

May he give you the desire of your heart
and make all your plans succeed.
We will shout for joy when you are victorious
and will lift up our banners in the name of
our God.
May the LORD grant all your requests.

PSALM 20:4–5

Have faith in the LORD your God and you will be upheld; have faith in his prophets and you will be successful.

2 CHRONICLES 20:20

Be on your guard; stand firm in the faith; be men of courage; be strong.

1 CORINTHIANS 16:13

And may these words of mine, which I have prayed before the Lord, be near to the Lord our God day and night, that he may uphold the cause of his servant and the cause of his people Israel according to each day's need, so that all the people of the earth may know that the Lord is God and that there is no other.

1 Kings 8:59–60

DEVOTIONAL THOUGHT ON SUSSESS

With everything imaginable working in his favor, it seemed Solomon would gratefully follow God. His prayer of dedication for the temple in 1 Kings 8 is one of the most majestic ever prayed.

Yet by the end of his reign Solomon had squandered away nearly every advantage. Along the way he lost sight of the original vision to which God had called him. Success in the kingdom of this world had crowded out interest in the kingdom of God. The brief, shining vision of a covenant nation faded away, and God withdrew his sanction. Solomon got whatever he wanted, especially when it came to symbols of power and status. Gradually, he depended less on God and more on the props around him: the world's largest harem, a house twice the size of the temple, an army well-stocked with chariots, a strong economy.

Success may have eliminated any crisis of disappointment with God, but it also seemed to eliminate Solomon's desire for God at all. The more he enjoyed the world's good gifts, the less he thought about the Giver.

Philip Yancey

GOD'S WORDS OF LIFE ON
THANKFULNESS

The trumpeters and singers joined in unison, as with one voice, to give praise and thanks to the LORD. Accompanied by trumpets, cymbals and other instruments, they raised their voices in praise to the LORD and sang: "He is good; his love endures forever."

2 CHRONICLES 5:13

Give thanks to the LORD, for he is good;
his love endures forever.

PSALM 106:1

Give thanks to the LORD, for he is good;
his love endures forever.
Let Israel say:
"His love endures forever."
Let the house of Aaron say:
"His love endures forever."

Let those who fear the LORD say:
*   "His love endures forever."*

PSALM 118:1–4

Give thanks to the LORD, for he is good.
*   "His love endures forever."*
Give thanks to the God of gods.
*   "His love endures forever."*
Give thanks to the Lord of Lords:
*   "His love endures forever."*

PSALM 136:1–3

The sounds of joy and gladness, the voices of bride and bridegroom, and the voices of those who bring thank offerings to the house of the LORD, saying,
*   "Give thanks to the LORD Almighty,*
*   for the LORD is good;*
*   his love endures forever."*

JEREMIAH 33:11

Give thanks to the LORD, for he is good;
*   his love endures forever.*

1 CHRONICLES 16:34

Let the peace of Christ rule in your hearts, since as members of one body you were called to peace. And be thankful. Let the word of Christ dwell in you richly as you teach and admonish one another with all wisdom, and as you sing psalms, hymns and spiritual songs with gratitude in your hearts to God. And whatever you do, whether in word or deed, do it all in the name of the Lord Jesus, giving thanks to God the Father through him.

COLOSSIANS 3:15–17

Devote yourselves to prayer, being watchful and thankful.

COLOSSIANS 4:2

[Job] said:
> "Naked I came from my mother's womb,
>   and naked I will depart.
> The LORD gave and the LORD has taken away;
>   may the name of the LORD be praised."

In all this, Job did not sin by charging God with wrongdoing.

JOB 1:21–22

> I will extol the LORD at all times;
>   his praise will always be on my lips.

PSALM 34:1

Do not be anxious about anything, but in everything, by prayer and petition, with thanksgiving, present your requests to God.

PHILIPPIANS 4:6

Give thanks in all circumstances, for this is God's will for you in Christ Jesus.

1 THESSALONIANS 5:18

But thanks be to God! He gives us the victory through our Lord Jesus Christ.

1 CORINTHIANS 15:57

Thanks be to God for his indescribable gift!

2 CORINTHIANS 9:15

Give thanks to the LORD, call on his name; make known among the nations what he has done.

1 CHRONICLES 16:8

Always giving thanks to God the Father for everything, in the name of our Lord Jesus Christ.

EPHESIANS 5:20

Praise the LORD.
I will extol the LORD with all my heart
in the council of the upright and in the assembly.
Great are the works of the LORD;
they are pondered by all who delight in them.

PSALM 111:1–2

[Be] rooted and built up in him, strengthened in the faith as you were taught, and overflowing with thankfulness.

COLOSSIANS 2:7

Sing to the LORD with thanksgiving;
make music to our God on the harp.

PSALM 147:7

Enter his gates with thanksgiving
and his courts with praise;
give thanks to him and praise his name.

PSALM 100:4

I will sacrifice a thank offering to you
and call on the name of the LORD.

PSALM 116:17

Therefore, since we are receiving a kingdom that cannot be shaken, let us be thankful, and so worship God acceptably with reverence and awe.

HEBREWS 12:28

For everything God created is good, and nothing is to be rejected if it is received with thanksgiving.

1 TIMOTHY 4:4

Through Jesus, therefore, let us continually offer to God a sacrifice of praise—the fruit of lips that confess his name.

HEBREWS 13:15

For the LORD your God will bless you in all your harvest and in all the work of your hands, and your joy will be complete.

DEUTERONOMY 16:15

DEVOTIONAL THOUGHT ON THANKFULNESS

The magic of a thankful spirit is that it has the power to replace . . .

anger with love,
resentment with happiness,
fear with faith,
worry with peace,
the desire to dominate
with the wish to play on a team,
self-preoccupation
with concern for the needs of others,
guilt with an open door to forgiveness,
sexual impurity
with honor and respect,
jealousy with joy at another's success,
lack of creativity
with inspired productivity,
inferiorities with dignity,
a lack of love
with an abundance of self-sharing.

Donald E. Demaray

GOD'S WORDS OF LIFE ON
TRUST

Those who know your name will trust in you,
for you, LORD, have never forsaken those who
seek you.

PSALM 9:10

Yet he did not waver through unbelief regarding the promise of God, but was strengthened in his faith and gave glory to God, being fully persuaded that God had power to do what he had promised.

ROMANS 4:20–21

Taste and see that the LORD is good;
blessed is the man who takes refuge in him.

PSALM 34:8

O LORD Almighty,
blessed is the man who trusts in you.

PSALM 84:12

Those who trust in the LORD are like Mount Zion,
which cannot be shaken but endures forever.

PSALM 125:1

Blessed is he whose help is the God of Jacob,
whose hope is in the LORD his God.

PSALM 146:5

Whoever gives heed to instruction prospers,
and blessed is he who trusts in the LORD.

PROVERBS 16:20

Blessed is the man who trusts in the LORD,
whose confidence is in him.
He will be like a tree planted by the water
that sends out its roots by the stream.
It does not fear when heat comes;
its leaves are always green.
It has no worries in a year of drought
and never fails to bear fruit.

JEREMIAH 17:7–8

You will keep in perfect peace
*   him whose mind is steadfast,*
*   because he trusts in you.*
Trust in the LORD forever,
*   for the LORD, the LORD, is the Rock eternal.*

ISAIAH 26:3–4

The LORD longs to be gracious to you;
*   he rises to show you compassion.*
For the LORD is a God of justice.
*   Blessed are all who wait for him!*

ISAIAH 30:18

Hezekiah trusted in the LORD, the God of Israel. There was no one like him among all the kings of Judah, either before him or after him.

2 KINGS 18:5

The LORD's unfailing love
*   surrounds the man who trusts in him.*

PSALM 32:10

Anyone who trusts in God will never be put to shame.

ROMANS 10:11

Trust in the LORD and do good;
dwell in the land and enjoy safe pasture.
Delight yourself in the LORD
and he will give you the desires of your heart.
Commit your way to the LORD;
trust in him and he will do this:
He will make your righteousness shine like the dawn,
the justice of your cause like the noonday sun.

PSALM 37:3–6

Blessed is the man
who makes the LORD his trust,
who does not look to the proud,
to those who turn aside to false gods.

PSALM 40:4

Then Nebuchadnezzar said, "Praise be to the God of Shadrach, Meshach and Abednego, who has sent his angel and rescued his servants! They trusted in him and defied the king's command and were willing to give up their lives rather than serve or worship any god except their own God."

DANIEL 3:28

A greedy man stirs up dissension,
but he who trusts in the LORD will prosper.

PROVERBS 28:25

Be strong and take heart,
all you who hope in the LORD.

PSALM 31:24

Fear of man will prove to be a snare,
but whoever trusts in the LORD is kept safe.

PROVERBS 29:25

When you pass through the waters,
I will be with you;
and when you pass through the rivers,
they will not sweep over you.
When you walk through the fire,
you will not be burned;
the flames will not set you ablaze.

ISAIAH 43:2

The LORD is good,
a refuge in times of trouble.
He cares for those who trust in him.

NAHUM 1:7

The LORD bless you
>and keep you;
the LORD make his face shine upon you
>and be gracious to you;
the LORD turn his face toward you
>and give you peace.

NUMBERS 6:24–26

To you, O LORD,
>I lift up my soul;
in you I trust, O my God.
>Do not let me be put to shame,
>nor let my enemies triumph over me.
No one whose hope is in you
>will ever be put to shame.

PSALM 25:1–3

Trust in the LORD with all your heart
>and lean not on your own understanding;
in all your ways acknowledge him,
>and he will make your paths straight.

PROVERBS 3:5–6

Offer right sacrifices
and trust in the Lord.
Many are asking, "Who can show us any good?"
Let the light of your face shine upon us, O Lord.
You have filled my heart with greater joy
than when their grain and new wine abound.
I will lie down and sleep in peace,
for you alone, O Lord, *make me dwell in safety.*

Psalm 4:5–8

DEVOTIONAL THOUGHT ON TRUST

We used to play a game at summer camp in which we would blindfold one of the kids and have him or her run through a wooded area, relying on a friend for verbal directions to help navigate. "Turn to the left; there's a tree coming!" "There's a log in front of you—jump!" Some kids would not trust the verbal directions whatsoever. They would shuffle their feet and walk very slowly, even though their friends were shouting that the way was clear. Other kids would trot along, and a few would go like gangbusters.

As Christians, we sometimes feel like those blindfolded children. We are not alone in the woods, though—God will direct our paths. But quite often his leadings sound illogical, irrational, countercultural. Sometimes he is so challenging that I say, "No, I think I'll just crawl back into my shell and play it safe." Then a voice inside me says, "Where's your courage, Hybels? Get up and walk. You can trust God."

It takes enormous courage to follow God's leadings in the Christian life. Some of his callings demand the best that you can summon. Some of his tests stretch you to the limit. Truly, spiritual courage or trust is on the endangered character-quality list.

Bill Hybels

Six days do your work, but on the seventh day do not work, so that your ox and your donkey may rest and the slave born in your household, and the alien as well, may be refreshed.

EXODUS 23:12

From the fruit of his lips a man is filled with good
things
as surely as the work of his hands rewards him.

PROVERBS 12:14

May the favor of the LORD our God rest upon us;
establish the work of our hands for us—
yes, establish the work of our hands.

PSALM 90:17

Lazy hands make a man poor,
but diligent hands bring wealth.

PROVERBS 10:4

Whatever your hand finds to do, do it with all your might, for in the grave, where you are going, there is neither working nor planning nor knowledge nor wisdom.

ECCLESIASTES 9:10

The lazy man does not roast his game,
but the diligent man prizes his possessions.

PROVERBS 12:27

The sluggard craves and gets nothing,
but the desires of the diligent are fully satisfied.

PROVERBS 13:4

All hard work brings a profit,
but mere talk leads only to poverty.

PROVERBS 14:23

The laborer's appetite works for him;
his hunger drives him on.

PROVERBS 16:26

The plans of the diligent lead to profit
as surely as haste leads to poverty.

PROVERBS 21:5

Do you see a man skilled in his work?
He will serve before kings;
he will not serve before obscure men.

PROVERBS 22:29

My heart took delight in all my work, and this was the reward for all my labor.

ECCLESIASTES 2:10

Sow your seed in the morning, and at evening let not your hands be idle, for you do not know which will succeed, whether this or that, or whether both will do equally well.

ECCLESIASTES 11:6

Make it your ambition to lead a quiet life, to mind your own business and to work with your hands, just as we told you, so that your daily life may win the respect of outsiders and so that you will not be dependent on anybody.

1 THESSALONIANS 4:11–12

For even when we were with you, we gave you this rule: "If a man will not work, he shall not eat."

2 THESSALONIANS 3:10

By the sweat of your brow you will eat your food until you return to the ground, since from it you were taken; for dust you are and to dust you will return.

GENESIS 3:19

Do not take advantage of a hired man who is poor and needy, whether he is a brother Israelite or an alien living in one of your towns. Pay him his wages each day before sunset, because he is poor and is counting on it. Otherwise he may cry to the LORD against you, and you will be guilty of sin.

DEUTERONOMY 24:14–15

The man who had received the five talents brought the other five. "Master," he said, "you entrusted me with five talents. See, I have gained five more." His master replied, "Well done, good and faithful servant! You have been faithful with a few things; I will put you in charge of many things. Come and share your master's happiness!"

MATTHEW 25:20–21

Now when a man works, his wages are not credited to him as a gift, but as an obligation.

ROMANS 4:4

DEVOTIONAL THOUGHT ON WORK

Many workers today are sacrificing themselves on the altar of work. They tolerate immensely harmful symptoms such as anger, chemical dependencies and loneliness in a blind pursuit of self-fulfillment through career success. This may be pathological—but it is also idolatrous! Such a person worships his career as though it were a god.

But like all idols, work is impotent in the face of true human need. I have sat with grown men, exceptionally powerful men in business, and watched them weep as they told me their tragic stories, some with personal lives shattered, others with families in shambles, perhaps their character debased or their circumstances out of control. None of their professional accomplishments, none of the machinery of their companies, none of their wealth is of the slightest help. They are in deep trouble and their god is impotent.

I grieve with such men. I also respect the fact that the same thing could happen to me as to anyone. It happens when we take God's gift of work and begin to worship and serve it rather than Christ.

Doug Sherman and William Hendricks

NOTES

13   152-153   (165)   Fin

(18)   36   96

Required   38

69

147

150

LORD REQUIRES   18   69   147

FRUITS of SPIRIT   165   96

1st & 2nd Commandments   36

NOTES